The
Polish
Americans

Other books in the
Immigrants in America series:

COVENTRY PUBLIC LIBRARY

The
Polish
Americans

By Meg Greene

LUCENT
BOOKS®

THOMSON

GALE

San Diego • Detroit • New York • San Francisco • Cleveland • New Haven, Conn. • Waterville, Maine • London • Munich

On cover: Dressed in traditional costumes, local Polish Americans parade with colorful cut-paper decorations at a festival in Tampa.

© 2004 by Lucent Books. Lucent Books is an imprint of The Gale Group, Inc., a division of Thomson Learning, Inc.

Lucent Books® and Thomson Learning™ are trademarks used herein under license.

For more information, contact
Lucent Books
27500 Drake Rd.
Farmington Hills, MI 48331-3535
Or you can visit our Internet site at http://www.gale.com

LIBRARY OF CONGRESS CATALOGING-IN-PUBLICATION DATA

Greene, Meg.
    Polish Americans / by Meg Greene.
       p. cm. — (Immigrants in America)
Summary: Reviews the reasons why millions of Poles have immigrated to America, what their passage was like, the kind of jobs most found, communities they formed, and the discrimination they faced.
Includes bibliographical references and index.
    ISBN 1-59018-516-1 (hardcover : alk. paper)
     1. Polish Americans—History—Juvenile literature. 2. Polish Americans—Social conditions—Juvenile literature. 3. Immigrants—United States—History—Juvenile literature. 4. Poland—Emigration and immigration—History—Juvenile literature. 5. United States—Emigration and immigration—History—Juvenile literature. [1. Polish Americans. 2. Immigrants. 3. United States—Emigration and immigration. 4. Poland—Emigration and immigration.] I. Title. II. Series.
    E184.P7G725 2004
    305.891'85073—dc21
                                          2003011233

Printed in the United States of America

CONTENTS

FOREWORD

Immigrants have come to America at different times, for different reasons, and from many different places. They leave their homelands to escape religious and political persecution, poverty, war, famine, and countless other hardships. The journey is rarely easy. Sometimes, it entails a long and hazardous ocean voyage. Other times, it follows a circuitous route through refugee camps and foreign countries. At the turn of the twentieth century, for instance, Italian peasants, fleeing poverty, boarded steamships bound for New York, Boston, and other eastern seaports. And during the 1970s and 1980s, Vietnamese men, women, and children, victims of a devastating war, began arriving at refugee camps in Arkansas, Pennsylvania, Florida, and California, en route to establishing new lives in the United States.

Whatever the circumstances surrounding their departure, the immigrants' journey is always made more difficult by the knowledge that they leave behind family, friends, and a familiar way of life. Despite this, immigrants continue to come to America because, for many, the United States represents something they could not find at home: freedom and opportunity for themselves and their children.

No matter what their reasons for emigrating, where they have come from, or when they left, once here, nearly all immigrants face considerable challenges in adapting and making the United States their new home. Language barriers, unfamiliar surroundings, and sometimes hostile neighbors make it difficult for immigrants to assimilate into American society. Some Vietnamese, for instance, could not read or write in their native tongue when they arrived in the United States. This heightened their struggle to communicate with employers who demanded they be literate in English, a language vastly different from their own. Likewise, Irish immigrant school children in Boston faced classmates who teased and belittled their lilting accent. Immigrants from Russia often felt isolated, having settled in areas of the United States where they had no access to traditional Russian foods. Similarly, Italian families, used to certain wines and spices, rarely shopped or traveled outside of New York's Little Italy, a self-contained community cut off from the rest of the city.

Even when first-generation immigrants do successfully settle into life in the United States, their children, born in America, often have different values and are influenced more by their country of birth than their parents' traditions. Children want to be a part of the American culture and usually welcome American ideals, beliefs, and styles. As they become more Americanized—adopting western dating habits and fashions, for instance—they tend to cast aside or even actively reject the traditions embraced by their parents. Assimilation, then, often becomes an ideological dispute that creates conflict among immigrants of every ethnicity. Whether Chinese, Italian, Russian, or Vietnamese, young people battle their elders for respect, individuality, and freedom, issues that often would not have come up in their homeland. And no matter how tightly the first generations hold on to their traditions, in the end, it is usually the young people who decide what to keep and what to discard.

The Immigrants in America series fully examines the immigrant experience. Each book in the series discusses why the immigrants left their homeland, what the journey to America was like, what they experienced when they arrived, and the challenges of assimilation. Each volume includes discussion of triumph and tragedy, contributions and influences, history and the future. Fully documented primary and secondary source quotations enliven the text. Sidebars highlight interesting events and personalities. Annotated bibliographies offer ideas for additional research. Each book in this dynamic series provides students with a wealth of information as well as launching points for further discussion.

INTRODUCTION

A Second Polish History

In the spring of 1899 Waclaw Kruszka, a young Roman Catholic priest from Poland, traveled to Wisconsin. Although the purpose of his visit was to meet with other Catholic Church officials throughout the state, Kruszka was also curious to see how Polish immigrants had fared in the United States. Kruszka, who went on to write a history of the Poles in America, reflected on his experience and that of his countrymen in their new home:

> In which corner . . . [of the United States] do you not find Poles? You will find them everywhere. Not only on fertile land, they multiply even on sand and rocks. . . . It would also be extremely difficult if not downright impossible to enumerate all the cities, towns, nooks and crannies inhabited by Poles. Counting grains of sand on the seashore or counting stars in the sky could not be more difficult. . . . Life sticks to everything that it can and a tree will grow on a bare rock, [and it] can also be said about the life of the Poles: there is no desert where Polish life could not exist.[1]

Here, There, Everywhere

Father Kruszka may have exaggerated the

number and diversity of places in which Poles could be found in the United States. Yet between 1850 and 1918 almost 2.5 million Poles, including Kruszka, arrived in the United States, making the Poles one of the largest groups of immigrants ever to come to the country. According to the 2000 census more than 9 million Americans claim Polish ancestry, marking them as the ninth largest ethnic group in the United States. Estimates further suggest that 75 percent of the North American population of Polish descent live in the United States. Well into the twentieth century, Poles continued to arrive in large numbers. From the 1940s until the 1990s, approximately 230,000 Polish immigrants made their way to the United States, many of them political refugees.

Father Kruszka was right to suggest that Polish Americans could be found in all regions of the United States, though the vast majority settled in the Midwest. In both Michigan and Wisconsin, for example, Polish Americans currently total almost 10 percent of the population. Large numbers of Polish Americans, though, have also made their homes in the Northeast, chiefly in New York, New Jersey, and Massachusetts. Florida and California have growing Polish American populations. Detroit, Chicago, Milwaukee, Los

Rescued from Nazi Germany, Polish children arrive in New York harbor. Since the nineteenth century, Poles have come to the United States to escape hardships in their homeland.

Angeles, and Cleveland have large Polish American enclaves. In recent years the number of Polish Americans living in Colorado, Arizona, and Nevada has surged.

Why They Came

The Polish immigrants who came to America beginning in the late nineteenth century were fleeing an unbearable existence in their homeland. By the late eighteenth century, three of the great powers of Europe, Austria, Prussia, and Russia had partitioned Poland three times. In 1772 the Austrians seized Galicia. The Prussians took northwestern Poland in 1793, while the Russians occupied eastern Poland in 1795. With these partitions Poland disappeared from the map of Europe and did not reappear until 1815 when the Congress of Vienna established the kingdom of Poland. Even then, however, Poland fell under the administration and control of Russia. The czars, Alexander I and after him his brother Nicholas I, imposed harsh restrictions upon the Poles. These restrictions included the suppression of the Polish language and the abolition of courses in Polish literature and history taught in classrooms. For the Russians, economic and political domination were not enough; nothing less than the complete cultural domination of the Polish people would satisfy the czar and his advisers in St. Petersburg.

During the first half of the nineteenth century, a number of Polish revolutionaries visited America. They believed that the United States was the model of a free society, which they desperately sought to imitate at home. When in 1863 a major uprising failed to overthrow czarist rule and achieve Polish independence, many revolutionary Poles became political exiles, seeking asylum in France, England, or the United States. In time their reports of life in America found their way to Poland. Nevertheless, the number of Poles in the United States remained comparatively small until the mid- to late nineteenth century.

The First Wave

The Poles have been a presence in America since the arrival in 1607 of several Polish artisans traveling with the first group of English settlers to Jamestown, Virginia. However, it was not until the late nineteenth century that large numbers of Polish immigrants began coming to the United States. The first wave of Polish immigration began approximately at the end of the American Civil War in 1865 and ended around 1920. Many of the immigrants who came during this period were known as *a za chlebam*, or "bread emigrants," because they came to America seeking economic opportunity. Attracted by tales of the great fortunes to be made, thousands of Poles immigrated to the United States. Their numbers were so great that by 1899 they ranked fourth among new arrivals to America. In 1900, 10 percent of all immigrants to the United States were Polish.

Poor and oppressed by their more powerful neighbors, Prussia, Austria, and Russia, the Poles who departed for America in the first wave came in search of jobs and

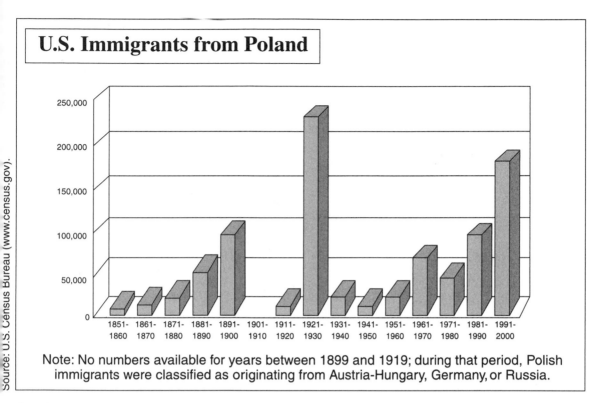

U.S. Immigrants from Poland

Source: U.S. Census Bureau (www.census.gov).

Note: No numbers available for years between 1899 and 1919; during that period, Polish immigrants were classified as originating from Austria-Hungary, Germany, or Russia.

freedom. Many dreamed of owning their own land to farm. Young men fled to avoid military service in the Russian or Austrian armies. Communists and other radicals left to escape arrest. Still others were weary of the political unrest and instability that accompanied foreign occupation. For thousands of Polish Jews, America was a symbol of religious freedom, and many came for the opportunity to practice their religion and way of life without fear of persecution.

The Second Wave

By the mid-1920s, however, the flood of Polish immigrants had slowed to a trickle. In 1921 and 1924 the U.S. Congress had enacted laws that severely restricted immigration, especially of Africans, Asians,

and southern and eastern Europeans. No fewer than ninety-five thousand Poles passed through the gates of Ellis Island in 1921; by 1925 the number permitted to enter the country had dwindled to five thousand per year.

After the Second World War, which ended in 1945, the number of Polish immigrants again swelled. This second wave lasted until 1980. Compared with other European countries, Poland suffered some of the greatest devastation and loss of life during the war, which claimed approximately 7 million Polish lives, or one-fifth of the entire population. Of those who survived, hundreds of thousands had lost their homes and, when the war ended, had no place to go.

With the passage of the Displaced Persons Act in 1948, the U.S. government made it easier for these refugees to come to America. With the Soviet occupation of Poland and Eastern Europe and the onset of the Cold War in the years that followed the Second World War, many Poles fled their homeland to escape communism.

These new immigrants differed from the first wave. Most had come from cities instead of rural districts. The second wave of immigrants was also made up of men and women who were educated and skilled.

The Third Wave

The third wave of Polish immigration began in 1980 and continues today. The number of immigrants grew during the 1980s after the Soviet regime attempted to suppress the Polish Solidarity Movement, which called for independence. Before entering the United States, many of these newcomers had to prove that they were political refugees. Like the refugees from the Second World War who came to America, a large number of these new immigrants are educated professionals.

Like the first generation of Polish immigrants, the majority of these men and women have come to America to work. Unlike most of their ancestors, however, many among the current generation did not intend to remain permanently in the United States. They had entered the country on visitors' visas, leaving their families in Poland. All, however, wished to im-

Polish American girls march in New York's annual Pulaski Day parade. Most Polish Americans strive to keep their cultural traditions alive.

prove their circumstances and their prospects in the United States, whether they intended to live here or to stay only a short time.

The Second Polish History

In 1901 one observer noted, the Polish immigrants to the United States had "a beautiful future . . . awaiting them . . . , and I guarantee this to you, that here in America, a 'Second Polish History will begin.'"[2] For many Polish immigrants, their personal history in America is deeply intertwined with the history of the nation at large. Certainly American industry, agriculture, society, and culture have benefited from their efforts and their talents.

In coming to America the Polish immigrants also brought with them important cultural values that have blended well with American norms. These traits include a devotion to family; a desire for property, respectability, and social status; and a strong belief in self-reliance. These characteristics, along with the determination to succeed and assimilate, aided the Polish immigrants in their transition to becoming American citizens.

During the course of the twentieth century, Polish immigrants built new communities in the United States, bringing with them their customs, culture, institutions, and cuisine. During that time Polish Americans have had to wrestle with tensions that separated the Old World from the New. Much has changed since the arrival of the first wave of immigrants. Today Polish Americans debate what it means to be Polish and American in ways that never occurred to a people engaged in a daily struggle to survive. But contemporary Polish Americans have not lost track of their ancestors or their history or their people, as they look for new ways to keep alive the memory of their homeland and of those who first left it to come to America.

CHAPTER ONE

Stary Kraj (The Old Country)

Poland has had a troubled history. Often conquered and occupied, Poland has endured chronic political instability and economic underdevelopment. Moreover, with little in the way of industrial development, the Poles have depended largely on agriculture to survive. Cities were few and small; those that did exist were located mainly along the Baltic Sea or in the industrialized regions of Silesia. The majority of Poles lived in the countryside. Yet in a country where land was often the sole source of income, wealth, and status, many Poles were "land poor." They had few opportunities to buy and own the land that they worked.

Poles, too, found themselves living under strict laws that their conquerors had imposed—laws that discriminated against them. By the late nineteenth century the relentless poverty and oppression, which showed no sign of ending, prompted many Poles to look to the United States as an escape from their misery and the *Stary Kraj*, the Old Country.

"People of the Fields"

Poland, which means "People of the Fields," is located in the heart of Europe. It is not a large country by comparison to its neighbors such as Russia or the former

Austrian Empire. The total land mass of Poland is 120,727 square miles, equal to an area roughly the size of Nevada. Surrounding Poland are Germany to the west, the Czech Republic and Slovakia (formerly part of the Austrian Empire) to the south, Russia and Lithuania to the north, and Belarus and Ukraine to the east. The Baltic Sea lies to the north and provides ready access to the Atlantic Ocean.

The geography of Poland is diverse, ranging from the lowlands in the central part of the country to sand dunes and swamps along the Baltic coast to the majestic Carpathian Mountains in the south. More than half of Poland is suitable for farming, particularly in the southern part of the country where the soil is rich and where, for many years, Polish farmers grew a variety of crops, including beets, potatoes, and wheat.

The Golden Age

At the beginning of the sixteenth century, Poland entered what many historians have called "The Golden Age." It became one of the largest and most powerful kingdoms in Europe, thanks to a succession of wise and capable monarchs. Poland developed a rich cultural heritage that influenced the renaissance of culture, literature, and art that characterized much of Europe during the 1500s. In addition, Poland had one of the most enlightened policies of religious tolerance. This policy led many Jews throughout Europe, who faced religious discrimination and persecution, to seek refuge in Poland, where the rulers welcomed them.

Poland also created one of the most representative governments in Europe. Beginning in 1572 the Poles abolished hereditary monarchy. Monarchs gained the throne only if elected by the ruling body known as the *Sejm*. This two-house legislature was composed of a senate, which included the powerful landowners and the clergy, and a lower house made up of the lesser nobles and smaller landowners. As a result, Polish monarchs, although powerful, were not absolute rulers like many European monarchs

Life Under the Manorial System

The manorial system was introduced into Poland during the fourteenth century by the German knights who had come to free Poland from Prussian invaders. Under this system land was divided into self-sufficient estates. These estates were held and looked after by the lord of the manor, often a member of the Polish nobility. The land on the estates was farmed by the peasants of the local village. In return for their labors the lord owed military protection to the peasants. The peasant never owned the land outright; rather it was "loaned" to the peasant by the lord. In addition to working the land, peasants were also charged dues, or taxes, on the land as well as on the peasant's level of productivity and any additional services that the lord provided. However, under the manorial system, the lord did not have the right to withdraw the property or to increase the dues or taxes.

The peasantry was now enslaved to the land. When not tending the lord's fields, serfs had other duties to see to, such as building barns, digging ditches, or repairing fences. Though the serfs could not be bought and sold like slaves, they were still restricted in many ways. They could not leave the manor or marry someone from another manor without the lord's permission. The lord could, if he chose, also try the serfs in his own court. In many cases the laws of the lord were the only legal recourse open to the serf. Thus the lord could, and often did, have complete control of the lives and property of his serfs.

who ruled with complete control over their countries. The Polish kings shared the power of governing the country with the clergy, the nobles, and the landowners. If a ruler tried to consolidate his power, exceed his authority, or violate the law, the assembly moved to restrain him.

Despite this enlightened arrangement, the kingdom of Poland was in trouble. The system of government made for a powerful nobility, who helped shape domestic and foreign policy. They also maintained a tight grip on their own lands and jealously guarded their aristocratic rights and privileges. The separation of powers, which restrained the monarch and protected the interests of the nobility, also led to mistrust, bickering, and division that actually weakened Poland, making it ripe for invasion and conquest. Throughout the seventeenth century, in a period of Polish history known as "The Deluge," Poles continually had to fend off attacks from Sweden, then counted among the great military powers of Europe.

Another experiment in government also contributed to the internal instability of Poland. In 1652 the *Sejm* instituted the *liberum* veto, which allowed a single dissenting member of either the senate or the lower chamber to block passage of legislation. A single vote could also adjourn the *Sejm*, forcing the legislators to postpone action on important issues until the next session.

The End of the Golden Age

The *liberum* proved disastrous, for it potentially placed the fate of the kingdom into the hands of one disgruntled member of the *Sejm*. The policy also made the government susceptible to outside influences. A bribe could cause a nobleman to act against the best interests of the kingdom, leaving it vulnerable to foreign powers. For the next two centuries Poland thus suffered serious decline that had far-reaching consequences for the future.

The nobles added to Poland's troubles by insisting that they alone controlled the land and by resisting efforts to develop commerce and manufacturing, which might have given others the opportunity to gain wealth, influence, and power at the nobles' expense. By failing to encourage economic modernization, the nobility, intent upon protecting its own status, weakened the Polish economy. Such actions doomed the peasants to a life of oppression and hardship on land that was not their own. They in turn had little incentive to defend those whom they saw as the source of their misery. Certain groups, including the Jews, Germans, and Gypsies, also increasingly became the targets of discrimination, hostility, and violence. They, too, began to feel estranged from Poland, which had formerly proven so hospitable to them. As a result of these changes, tensions, and hostilities, Poland faced a mounting internal crisis that, in the end, contributed to its destruction at the hands of its enemies.

At the beginning of the eighteenth century, Poland was in chaos. The continual infighting among nobles had first wearied and finally decimated the people. The instability brought on by constant warfare made Poland a prime target for conquest by its land-hungry neighbors—Prussia, Russia, and Austria. Too busy with their own squabbles, the Polish nobility could not foresee, let alone prevent, the fate that was about to befall the kingdom.

A Disappearing Homeland

Beginning in 1772 the governments and armies of Prussia, Russia, and Austria dismantled and divided Poland. During the next fifty years Poland disappeared from the map of Europe, and the Poles could no longer control their fate and future. By the early nineteenth century, the former independent kingdom of Poland was gone, not to reappear until after the First World War, which ended in 1918.

The domination of Poland had a profound impact on Polish culture. Faced with the demand to adopt the languages and cultures of their conquerors, Poles, secretly laboring under the protection of the Roman Catholic Church, struggled to preserve their native language, history, culture, and identity. The bond between the Poles and the church grew even stronger than it had been, so much so that, for many Poles, being a patriot and a Catholic were one and the same. Persons could not be good Poles unless they were also good Catholics. This identification of being Polish with being Catholic continued among Poles who immigrated to the United States.

Amid the upheaval of foreign occupation, there remained a point of stability and unity within Poland: the manorial system, which helped the Polish nobility maintain its power. This institution, which dated back to the Middle Ages and

was no longer found in western Europe, had trapped the Poles in an insular and stagnant society. By the late eighteenth and early nineteenth centuries, however, the manorial system had begun to break down, setting in motion a series of events that propelled the first waves of Polish immigrants to depart for American shores.

A Country's Woes

By the beginning of the nineteenth century dramatic changes were taking place in Poland, transforming both its economic and social systems. The predominantly rural, agricultural society that had once been the foundation of the country was disrupted by a combination of factors that included an increase in population, the expansion of commercial agriculture, and the growth of transportation, industry, and cities. With these changes came the gradual dissolution of the traditional way of life of the Polish peasants. When the landlords consolidated their estates and adopted agricultural technology, they no longer needed the labor of their peasants. As a consequence they threw them off the land. By 1880 nearly 80 percent of the rural population in German-occupied Poland was unemployed. Some of these men and women found their way into Polish factories. Polish industry could not, however, absorb all of them. Those who could not find work eventually found their way to North America.

In Austrian-occupied Poland the situation was worse. Economic development in this part of Poland was stifled. Reliance

Partitions of Poland

LIVONIA

COURLAND

Baltic Sea

SAMOGITIA

ERMLAND

Gdánsk (1793)

EAST
PRUSSIA

**TO
RUSSIA**

LITHUANIA

RUSSIAN

POMERANIA

WEST
PRUSSIA

TO

WHITE RUSSIA

EMPIRE

PRUSSIA

SOUTH
PRUSSIA

NEW EAST
PRUSSIA

SILESIA

WESTERN
GALICIA

POLESIE

TO

VOLHYNIA

UKRAINE

AUSTRIA

NEW SILESIA

GALICIA AND LODOMERIA

PODOLIA

HUNGARY

TURKISH EMPIRE

First Partition (1772)

Second Partition (1793)

Third Partition (1795)

N

on outdated agricultural equipment and methods left the region technologically backward and its residents poor. Lack of proper fertilizer and an inefficient crop rotation system, for example, produced low crop yields even when the rains and the weather cooperated with farmers. In addition ethnic rivalries among the Poles, Ukrainians, Muslims, and Jews fueled social and political tensions that prevented residents from cooperating to solve common economic problems.

The czar's policies hampered the economic development of Russian-occupied Poland. To promote commercial agriculture, the czar encouraged diversification, that is, the growing of many different kinds of crops. If one crop endured a poor season, others might flourish. This method was preferred over the traditional three field method, in which two fields were used, with one field lying fallow, or unused. In growing more crops and using more land, the czar hoped to earn more monies for the Russian treasury as well as to make Poland the "breadbasket" for the Russian Empire.

To make even more money, the czar also instituted a policy that enabled landlords to charge exorbitant rents. If a peasant failed to pay, he lost the right to farm the land and was then evicted from the land by his landlord. This policy left thousands of peasants homeless and roaming the countryside looking for a place to live. The problem was further compounded when in 1864 the Russians emancipated the Polish serfs. This meant that any serf who no longer wished to work the land was free to leave. In their attempt to create a more profitable agricultural policy, the czar and his advisers had only succeeded in creating a large homeless and destitute population.

Compounding economic problems throughout Poland was the collapse of grain prices during the late nineteenth century. The ensuing agricultural depression threw thousands of laborers out of work as landowners seeking to cut costs employed fewer workers. To complicate matters, Poland had one of the highest birthrates in Europe at the time. Thus there were more

Poles to feed when grain production decreased dramatically. Thousands more peasants flocked to the growing cities in search of work, escalating pressure on a crumbling social and economic system.

The Heart of Industry

By the mid–nineteenth century, two industrial centers located in Russian-occupied Poland were flourishing: Warsaw and Lodz. Coal mining, iron, steel and textile manufacturing, and sugar refining had transformed these cities into successful industrial centers. In fact, the population of Lodz increased from 31,000 residents in 1860 to 314,000 persons in 1897. It was nicknamed the "Polish Manchester," a reference to the great industrial city in Great Britain.

These cities absorbed a great number of peasants into the work force. By 1904, however, with the outbreak of the Russo-Japanese War, the eastern markets that purchased large amounts of the manufactured goods produced in Warsaw and Lodz were closed. This caused a severe industrial depression in Poland. Worker unrest during the following year worsened the situation. The final blow came when the Russian monarchy decided to shift industrial production away from Poland and into Russia itself.

Repressive Regimes

In addition to economic hardship, the Poles were increasingly subject to discrimination, leading many to make the difficult decision to leave Poland for the

United States. Great numbers of Roman Catholic Poles, for example, elected to leave German-occupied Poland beginning in the 1870s as a result of policies designed to suppress the Roman Catholic Church. In 1898 one member of the *Reichstag*, or German Parliament, described the goal of the Prussian government as "not only to make loyal citizens of the Prussians of Polish nationality but also to transform them into Germans."[3] To accomplish that goal the Germans did everything from changing street signs and place names from Polish to German to taking control of Polish schools and encouraging Poles to adopt German names. In addition, the German government confiscated or bought lands from the Polish nobles with the express purpose of opening the lands up for German colonization. Beginning in 1886 and continuing for the next twenty-five years, approximately 150,000 Germans moved onto Polish lands.

In Russian-occupied Poland, Poles also suffered from harsh repressive policies. In addition to confiscating land, which was then sold to other Russians, the Russian government often took young boys and sent them to Russia where they would be educated in Russian military schools. While many of the boys were orphans, families of suspected radicals were also targeted. The assault on Polish culture was relentless. A Danish historian and literary critic visiting Poland in 1885 described the conditions he found there:

The Polish language is absolutely forbidden in the University. All lectures, no matter whether delivered by men of Russian or Polish birth, must be in Russian. Not even the history

Life in a Polish Village

The typical farm of the Polish peasant consisted of several strips of land scattered here and there, usually near a village. The average size of a peasant's farm was about five acres, but it was rare for the entire acreage to be all together. Instead a peasant's holdings might be scattered over as many as forty different locations. The land was held communally by the village, and the village council was responsible for assigning the plots of land to the residents of the village. The village commune also determined what a peasant family would grow on its acreage. Before World War I most Polish villages followed the traditional three-field system in which one-third of the land would be tilled for winter crops, such as wheat or other grains, and one-third for summer crops, such as potatoes or barley. The remaining months the field lay fallow, or unused. It was thought that this system allowed the fields to "rest" and stay fertile. In reality the system was inefficient and discouraged modernization to more efficient farming methods.

Shoppers stroll through a busy outdoor market in nineteenth-century Warsaw. By the early 1900s, Poland was mired in a serious economic depression.

of Polish literature may be taught in the language of the country. . . . Even in the corridors of the University the students are forbidden to speak Polish with each other. . . . So strict is the prohibition . . . that a boy twelve years of age was recently shut up for twenty-four hours in the dark because . . . he said to a comrade in Polish: "Let us go home together."[4]

The Jews were also targeted under the various regimes in partitioned Poland. Under the czar's regime, for instance, Jews faced in-

creasing economic restrictions, along with social, civic, and political sanctions. In Russia, violence against the Jews was sanctioned by Russian laws and encouraged in other ways. In Galicia, which held the largest number of Jews in Poland, anti-Semitism became more prevalent. Poles boycotted Jewish merchants and manufacturers, preferring instead to give their business to their Christian competitors. Incidents of violence also increased against the Jews, forcing many to leave the region for America.

During the partition years, moreover, thousands of young Polish boys and men faced mandatory military service in the Austrian, Russian, or the Prussian armies. Life in the military was uniformly hard, but particularly hard for the Polish recruits. Held in little regard by native-born soldiers, the conscripted Poles were forced into long terms of enlistment, which varied from four years of service in the Austrian army to six years in the Russian. The pay was nonexistent and living conditions were harsh. To escape from this unbearable nightmare, many young Polish men left for America.

Postwar Immigration

In the years following World War I, Polish immigration to the United States dropped dramatically as a result of the immigration quotas created by the U.S. government. Although fewer Poles were allowed to come into the country, immigration to the United States tapered off for other reasons, too. The arrival of the First World War had had a profound impact upon the Poles. Not only did the war prevent Polish emigrants from leaving, but thousands of Poles from what was viewed as a "surplus population" were killed. It was from this group that many Polish immigrants had come.

In the years following the First World War, Poland again became an independent nation, maintaining an uneasy peace with its neighbors, the Soviet Union and Germany. With the postwar reconstruction and the growth of industrialization in Poland came new employment opportunities as new factories and businesses appeared. As a result fewer Poles left their homeland.

Two Old Enemies Return

The peace and prosperity that Poland enjoyed was cut short, however. On September 1, 1939, the German army invaded Poland. Two weeks later, on September 17, the Soviet Union sent its army to invade Poland from the east. The Polish army fought bravely but was no match for the more advanced technology of the Germans and the sheer numbers of the Soviets. By October, Poland fell completely under the control of Nazi Germany and the Soviet Union, which held part of the country as the result of an agreement signed with Germany in August.

The Nazis quickly turned Poland into a killing field, in part to completely subdue and eradicate the Poles, whom the Germans had long believed were an inferior race. Hundreds of Catholic clergy, members of the Polish intellectual community, the Polish nobility, mayors, and lawyers were executed or sent to a concentration camp located near the village of Auschwitz. Over the next five years 860,000 Poles were sent to various regions of Nazi-occupied Europe to work in the labor camps or as slaves in war-related industries, while a total of 330,000 Poles were executed.

The Holocaust

The complete erasure of Poland as a nation and as a people was only one goal of Adolf Hitler, the leader of Nazi Germany. Another was the complete annihilation of the Jewish people. To that end, the Germans, beginning in 1933, enacted a system of programs designed to contain and eliminate European Jewry.

Because the largest concentration of Jews was in Poland, Hitler's mass extermination program began there. In the large-scale executions known today as the Holocaust, approximately 6 million Jews perished between the years 1933 and 1945. An additional 2.5 million Poles were deported either as slaves to Germany or as prisoners in concentration camps. In these camps they were tortured, worked to death, or simply murdered. By the end of the war in 1945, only about 100,000 Polish Jews had survived out of a population of 3.1 million. After the war, thousands of non-Jewish Poles were homeless refugees.

Many of these people came to America to start a new life.

Soviet Satellite

Yet the Poles were freed from one oppressor only to fall into the hands of another. The Soviet troops who had marched into Poland to "liberate" it from the Nazis soon established a Communist regime that ruled Poland for the next forty-five years. Because of the tight grip of the Communist government, few Poles were allowed to leave. When in the 1970s the Polish economy collapsed, the Soviet-style gov-

German soldiers invade Warsaw in early September 1939. Two weeks later, Soviet troops invaded Poland from the east.

The sign over the entrance gate at Auschwitz reads, "Work Brings Freedom." During the Holocaust, millions of Polish Jews were killed in concentration camps.

ernment stepped up a program of political repression and censorship in an effort to prevent further political unrest. One result was an increased number of Poles immigrating to the United States. With the collapse of the Communist regime in Poland in 1990, there was a slow but steady rise in the number of persons leaving the country. Times were still uncertain, and despite the withdrawal of Soviet forces following the destruction of the regime, many Poles hoped for better opportunities and the promise of a better life in America.

CHAPTER TWO

Looking Across the Ocean

From the nineteenth century on, Polish immigrants arrived in the United States at least somewhat acquainted with their new homeland. Many had learned of America through immigrant friends and relatives who had written letters home describing their new lives. For many Poles the possibility of owning their own land or finding a job that paid decent wages was a powerful incentive to leave Poland.

Later, agents for railroads, steamship lines, and various businesses came to Poland in search of prospective immigrants. They, too, advertised the great opportunities in America for all those bold enough to undertake the journey. In no time, agents promised, those who worked for a wage could save enough to buy land. The news was encouraging. In 1891 Polish farmworkers received an average of twelve cents a day, while American farm laborers earned ninety cents. This seemed like a fortune to most Poles.

Economic motives, however, were not solely responsible for prompting immigration. Others Poles were drawn to the United States because of the political, civil, and religious freedoms it offered. They came seeking asylum, or refuge, from the horrors of war, persecution, and political unrest.

Cast Adrift

If not for the far-reaching social and economic changes that took place in Poland after the middle of the nineteenth century, chances are that the first great wave of Polish immigration would not have taken place. As it was, the Poles were still among the last of the European peoples to come to the United States. Yet, when hundreds of thousands of Polish peasants found themselves suddenly expelled from the land, the decision to leave became simpler. To stay meant to starve.

For other Poles, especially those living in the areas under German, Austrian, or Russian control, immigrating to the United States also became a matter of cultural survival. Fearing the loss of their cherished customs, traditions, and language, many Poles looked to the United States as a place where they could live freely without fear.

A Shorter Journey

The relative ease of travel to America made the decision to leave easier. An improved system of transportation, including railroads and steamships, made the prospect of immigrating seem realistic, as simple as taking the train to the nearest sea-port. From there, steamships could carry people across the sea in a matter of days instead of months.

Although travel was expensive, sometimes costing the entire family income, it seemed worth the expense to bring the promise of American life within reach. As one Polish peasant living in Galicia wrote after watching the train rumble past his village: "This passing train . . . reminds us of our poverty here and tells us that somewhere else life is better, that the world is different, big, better."[5] Another Pole was

Steamships shortened the transatlantic journey for passengers like these from a matter of months to just days.

less positive but still favored taking a chance on the United States. "Whether we rot here or there," he wrote, "it's all the same to us. At any rate, we want to try our luck."[6] For this Pole, and for thousands of his countrymen, the attraction of America would be too great to ignore.

A Long-Standing Friendship

The Polish people have enjoyed a special friendship with America. For the Poles, the quest for an independent Poland has marked much of their history. It is little wonder, then, that the Poles took a special interest in watching the American colonists struggle for their independence against England. When the Revolutionary War began in 1775, many Poles were inspired to aid the American cause, which mirrored their own struggles for national independence, unity, and freedom.

Two of the most well-known Polish patriots who helped the Americans were Count Casimir Pulaski and Thaddeus Kosciuszko. Pulaski, the son of Polish nobles, was already on the run from Russian authorities for his part in an unsuccessful revolt against Russia in his own country. He escaped to Paris, where he met Benjamin Franklin. Franklin introduced Pulaski to General George Washington, commander in chief of the American forces. Under Pulaski's leadership the "Pulaski Legion," a group of light infantry and cavalry, helped the Americans win against the British in the South. Pulaski is often considered to be the "Father of the American Cavalry" for his skill and training of soldiers on horseback. Pulaski died in 1779 as the result of wounds he received during the battle for Savannah, Georgia.

Thaddeus Kosciuszko came to the Americans' aid in 1776. Kosciuszko, who came from a family with a distinguished military history, studied extensively at military schools in Poland and France. A trained military engineer, Kosciuszko offered his services to the Continental Congress and was assigned to the post of colonel of engineers. His many skills contributed to the Ameri-

"Birds of Passage"

Polish immigrants who traveled back and forth between Poland and the United States were known as "birds of passage." Often these men found seasonal types of work in America, such as construction or farming. When the job or season ended, they then returned to their villages in Poland where they would visit family and friends. Some men saved enough money to return home and marry and then come back to America to work again. For shipping companies and other businesses in America, the "birds of passage" were good advertisements as to how wonderful life in America really was. As a result, many Poles wishing to live the "good life" were persuaded to leave their villages and go to America, too.

cans' victory at Saratoga in 1777, which is considered by many historians to be the turning point of the American Revolution. For his service to the American people, Kosciuszko was awarded American citizenship. Kosciuszko later returned to Poland where he continued to fight for Polish independence.

During the middle of the nineteenth century, as the Polish quest for freedom continued, a number of Americans returned the favor by offering their support for the Polish cause. American writers such as Edgar Allan Poe offered to serve in the Polish army; others, such as James Fenimore Cooper, helped by raising funds to aid the Polish rebels. For Poles the word "democracy" held a special meaning. Although their efforts failed, Polish revolutionaries had planted the seed of freedom in Polish soil. By the late nineteenth century, when the first significant wave of Polish immigrants began arriving in the United States, they were already enamored with "the land of the free."

Thaddeus Kosciuszko played a key role in the American victory at Saratoga during the Revolutionary War.

A Spiritual Duty

American writer Louis E. Van Norman, who visited Poland in the early twentieth century, spent a day at a small village schoolhouse. While there, he witnessed a remarkable exchange, which he later described in his book *Poland, the Knight Among Nations:*

While in Zbaraz [Galicia] I visited a school for peasant children. Its sessions were held in a rustic little one-room building with the conventional thatched roof. . . . For my especial benefit, the prize scholar was asked where was America. He hesitated a moment, then he said he did not know, except that it was the country to which good Polish boys went when they died.[7]

Although it was not easy for Poles to leave their country, the image of America as an earthly paradise, was, in the end, irresistible. Yet there is another important aspect that helps to explain Polish attitudes toward immigration. In leaving Poland they sought to preserve the very things that they were leaving behind and that they held most dear: family, community, and a familiar way of life.

Traveling away from the village or leaving family behind had traditionally been unacceptable behavior among rural Poles. So to make the idea of leaving Poland less frightening, and perhaps to ease their guilt at going, Poles created a number of myths. In these stories devoutly Catholic Poles received guidance and blessing to leave from the Virgin Mary herself.

By attaching religious significance to their leaving, the Poles convinced themselves that they were carrying out a higher calling, a spiritual duty, to fulfill God's purpose for them on earth. The Poles were not leaving merely to better themselves, but because God had willed them to go. Leaving thus became not so much a choice as an obedient sacrifice. By coming to America, the Poles could tell themselves, they fulfilled the purpose that God had designed for them. America was their destiny.

"America Fever"

Popular stories about life in America combined with these spiritual myths attracted Poles to the United States. Beginning in the early 1850s, stories began to circulate throughout villages and towns about the "golden mountains" of America, a possible reference to the California gold rush

of 1848–1849. Besides these stories another popular legend told of "streets of gold" in American cities. If gold were so abundant that Americans paved their streets with it, then surely riches must await everyone who came to the United States.

Perhaps the best form of publicity for the United States was the many letters written from immigrants to relatives in Poland describing the opportunities that American society presented. These letters from America, noted a historian of immigration, were "treated like 'religious relics' in Polish villages; they electrified the countryside and gave rise to the obsession with emigration popularly known as 'America fever.'"[8] "Dear Parents," wrote one Polish immigrant, "always it will be better for you to live here [in the United States] than there [in Poland]. . . . If you're to break your back on some master's land, do it here on your own. . . . When I remember the misery at home my skin crawls." Another letter offered "a *shiffkarta* [a one-way ticket to the United States] because back home you're serving others from childhood and so it will be until your old age, but in America you can make something of yourself."[9]

Although employed as a scrubwoman in a Chicago hotel, one Polish immigrant still described her life in America with enthusiasm:

I am getting along very well, very well. I have worked in a factory and I am now working in a hotel. I receive 18 (in our money 32) dollars a month and that is very good. . . . We

Money Home

Poles were known to be thrifty. Those who had come to America were careful about saving their money in order either to return home or, in many cases, to save enough money to bring over family members or friends. But over time the amount of money sent back to Poland grew so large that American and European authorities worried about the impact. By 1910 it was estimated that approximately $40 million had been sent back to Poland by Polish immigrants in America. Galicia alone was estimated to be receiving on average between $4 and $5 million every year from immigrants. Money sent home had a great impact on the Polish economy, which many welcomed. But the U.S. government was not as pleased. In a report issued in 1907 the U.S. Immigration Commission, the forerunner of the U.S. Bureau of Immigration, stated that the new Polish immigrants, in sending their money back to Poland rather than spending it in America, were seriously weakening the American economy, a claim that was patently false.

eat here every day what we get only at Easter in our country. We are bringing over Helena and brother now. I have $120 and I sent back $90.[10]

Many immigrants remarked on what to them were the incredible wages that American workers earned. By 1891 unskilled laborers in the United States were earning $1.48 a day, a wage that was twelve times higher than that of the average worker in Poland. As one Pole observed, "For these minds accustomed to the poor local wages, it was like a fantasy, like a dream pay!"[11]

The flurry of letters did not escape the notice of the U.S. government. In 1907 an official for the U.S. Immigration Commission on Slavic Immigration wrote: "In the large majority of cases . . . the immediate inducement to emigrants to leave home and sail for America comes in the form of personal letters from friends or members of their own families already in the United States."[12]

Advertising the Good Life

Adding to this increased interest in America were the promotional ads that steamship companies placed to entice passengers. Some American states, particularly those in the Midwest, also printed pamphlets to be distributed at the shipping line offices or by immigrants returning to Poland for a visit. For instance, one such pamphlet from the state of Wisconsin advertised the following: "Come! In Wisconsin all men are free and equal before the law. . . . Religious freedom is absolute."[13]

Minnesota, by contrast, emphasized not only religious freedom but also economic prospects, boasting the availability of something that most Poles craved: land. In part, the Minnesota pamphlet read:

> To Laboring Men, who earn a livelihood by honest toil; to Landless Men who aspire to the dignity and independence which comes from possession in God's free earth; to All Men of moderate means, and men of wealth, who will accept homes in a beautiful and prosperous country. . . . It is well to exchange the tyrannies and thankless toil of the old world for the freedom and independence of the new . . . it is well for the hand of labour to bring forth the rich treasures hid in the bosom of the NEW EARTH.[14]

As attractive as owning land was for many Poles, others were drawn to high-paying industrial jobs in American factories, where they believed they could earn more money in a year than during a lifetime spent in Poland.

Like Warsaw (pictured), many Polish cities were devastated during World War II. Many refugees migrated to America as a result.

Postwar Emigration

Poles looked to America again after the end of World War II. Poland was in ruins; more than one-fifth, or 35 million, Europeans of Polish descent died during the course of the war. Many cities were littered with blackened rubble, and thousands of people were left without homes, food, water, or clothing. In addition, there were approximately 240,000 refugees. Many of them were Polish army veterans who were scattered about Europe and who did not want to go back home because of the Communists.

A number of Polish American organizations were created to help Polish refugees. They conducted fund-raisers to help relief efforts. The Polish American Congress lobbied the U.S. government to relax the immigration quotas so as to allow more Poles to come to America. With the passage of the Special Displaced Persons Act of 1948, the U.S. government relaxed the restrictive quotas placed on immigrants from Eastern Europe, making it possible for thousands of war refugees to come to America. The new legislation gave special priority to those immigrants with skills and to those wishing to rejoin family members. Under the new legislation 175,000 Polish refugees entered the United States between 1945 and 1954. Another 75,000 Poles came to the United States from 1955 to 1966.

By the mid-1960s, many of the new immigrants coming to America were younger. Most had grown up and had been educated in Communist Poland. Because of this their expectations of America were somewhat different from the expectations of the first and second waves of immigrants. Some of these new arrivals were dubbed "economic immigrants" because they had come for freedom and economic advancement.

Unlike the first wave who were largely uneducated and unskilled, these immigrants were often professionals who easily found jobs. In spite of enjoying the freedom of America, many of these immigrants were also very critical of American society, finding it to be almost too "free." In addition to the large number of professionals who immigrated to the United States, there were a number of students who came to live and study. Unlike the earlier immigrants, none ever expected to return to Poland.

For these Poles and thousands of others before them the lure of America was too great to ignore. While immigrants had different reasons for coming, they all sought, in one way or another, the freedom to pursue their dreams. The question for many, however, was how best to go about getting to America.

CHAPTER THREE

To America

The decision to immigrate was only the beginning. Despite the uncertainty that awaited them, thousands of Polish men, women, and children undertook the journey with a sense of optimism. As one historian of immigration has written of this first wave of Polish immigrants,

> It was not exclusively a movement of the "huddled masses" or only of the "tired and yearning to breathe free," as Emma Lazarus' poem inscribed on the base of the Statue of Liberty would have it, but rather a movement of the young, the ener-

getic, the confident, and the adventurous.[15]

The first Polish immigrants came mainly from the Austrian-occupied territory of Galicia. Between 1880 and 1900 the number of Polish immigrants from this area rose from 82,000 to 340,000. Although their backgrounds were varied and diverse, the Galicians who came to America were predominantly displaced farmworkers who had been turned off the land or farmworkers who sought better opportunities. A sizeable percentage, perhaps as many as half, of these immigrants planned to stay for only a short time in the United States; others came with every intention of settling permanently in America. As Polish immigrant Walter Mrozowski, who came to the United States in 1905, recalls,

I decided I would go to America. I had heard about the United States and what a grand country it was. I had enough money to pay my way. . . . I was leaving my homeland and relatives, but I had made up my mind. Nothing could stop me from seeing the United States. Anyway, after the boat headed for this country, I knew I had to go along with it.[16]

The High Cost of a Dream

Making the trip to America was not cheap. To raise the money for passage, many Poles sold off their land (if they

European immigrants huddle on board the deck of a steamship headed for America. Most Polish immigrants came to the United States in search of economic opportunity.

How Many Poles?

While historians know a great deal about Polish immigration to America, there is still some question about how many native Poles arrived during the first great wave of immigration. Part of the confusion results from the U.S. census and how it recorded national origin. Prior to 1885 immigration officials did not list Poland as a person's official "country of birth" because during the partition years Poland did not officially exist. What this meant was that a person born in territory that had once been the kingdom of Poland would be classified as German, Austrian, or Russian, depending on the country that controlled the immigrant's native region at the time. Even when Poland officially existed as a country, foreign-born immigrants who settled in Poland had to choose a country of birth. Such immigrants did not identify themselves as Polish, but the government classified them as being of Polish origin. In a revised study done during the 1970s, when historians looked again at the immigration numbers during the period from 1899 to 1932, it was estimated that approximately 1,443,473 "official" Poles, that is, Poles born in Poland, came to the United States.

owned any), livestock, and personal items. Besides money for passage, all immigrants entering the United States had to have at least twenty-five dollars with them. Those who had no money and little or nothing to sell borrowed to pay for the tickets. The interest rates on such loans, whether secured from a moneylender or a steamship company, were often illegally high.

The high cost of passage sometimes prompted one male member of a family to go to America first, with the understanding that he would get a job and send a portion of his earnings to those still in Poland so that they might join him as soon as possible. Friends also sent money to Poland so that others from their town, village, or neighborhood could afford to make the journey to the United States.

There were a number of ways in which potential immigrants could arrange and pay for their transport. Many first-time travelers made arrangements through a bank, which could book passage for them and also receive their payment. People could employ "professional immigrants." These were usually men who had been to America several times. Working with agents of the shipping lines, they acted as recruiters, visiting villages and towns to identify potential immigrants. The recruiters received a fee for their services from the steamship companies for every passenger they found. They also traveled with immigrants, making sure, in theory at least, that all of them reached their destination safely.

The "Landsmen"

For prospective immigrants, the number of details—financial, legal, and other—that had to be taken care of before they left was overwhelming. Such complications made the agents who represented steamship lines all the more vital. Known as "landsmen" because they served the area from which they came, these agents were indispensable in preparing immigrants for their journey to America.

Landsmen operated much in the same way as a travel agent. They were located in major cities; port cities, in particular, were an obvious favorite. Through the landsman the immigrants purchased their tickets. The landsman then provided each immigrant with a "ship's card," which functioned as a boarding pass, to show they had paid their passage. For those having to travel to reach a port city, the landsman arranged for the purchase and mailing of railroad tickets.

While many landsmen were honest and did their best to help immigrants with their travel arrangements, there were others who were unscrupulous and motivated by greed. More concerned with getting immigrants' money than with assisting them, some landsmen resorted to fraud. Many prospective immigrants found out too late that their tickets were no good. By the time they learned the sad truth, their corrupt agents had disappeared, and the disappointed travelers were not only out of money but also out of luck. They would have to postpone or cancel the journey to America.

In this cartoon from the late 1800s, crafty steamship agents take advantage of naive Polish emigrants.

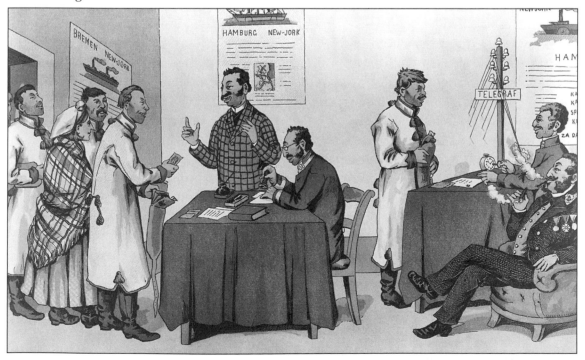

Preparing for the Journey

The steamship companies also helped immigrants prepare for their voyage. Like the landsmen, however, the shipping companies could not always guarantee that an immigrant would actually be able to enter America. As a result the steamship companies took a much closer interest in the welfare of the immigrant. This interest was not based on a genuine concern for the immigrant's well-being; rather it was a question of how much a company stood to make from the voyage.

Because of the increasingly restrictive immigration laws passed in the United States, steamship lines assumed responsibility to care for the immigrants before and during the journey. In addition, the companies bore the cost of deporting an immigrant who could not meet the physical or mental requirements for entering the United States. If American immigration officials rejected too many passengers from a voyage, the losses could be considerable. In 1903, for each immigrant U.S. officials turned away, companies were fined only $10, which for some ship lines was a small penalty to pay. But by 1905 the fine had risen to $100 for each immigrant barred from entering the United States. By this time the companies had learned that if they wished to profit from transporting immigrants, it was wise policy to take good care of them so that they were as healthy as possible upon arrival.

To ensure the passengers' health, the steamship companies hired physicians to provide physical examinations of every prospective immigrant. If the doctors pro-nounced them healthy and fit for travel, the company required a deposit toward the purchase of a steerage ticket, the full price of which averaged between $30 to $36, or the equivalent of $629 to $754 in today's currency. Upon receipt of the deposit, company agents issued a certificate stating a reservation had been made in that person's name.

Leaving Home

In the days before departure, travelers were busy packing. Some immigrants, such as Martha Konwicki who came to America with her mother, brother, and sister in 1913, took only the most basic necessities. As she recalls, "We couldn't take much because my mother had the three of us that she had to take care of and everything was left behind in Warsaw, valuable things we had . . . we left everything behind—we just took clothes."[17] Celia Rypinski, who was only twelve years old when she made the journey to America, had even less: "I did not even have underwear, but lived in two shirts. . . . [My stepmother] gave me old torn shoes and her skirt—that's what I had for my better clothes."[18]

For other immigrants, the primary concern was to settle their affairs. If a Pole had land or a home, this was placed in the hands of a relative. Farm livestock, if any was owned, was sold to help pay for the cost of the trip. Some immigrants even parted with family treasures in order to raise enough funds for traveling. Merchants closed up shops or turned their businesses over to someone else. For

Catholic Poles it was particularly important to go to mass and be blessed by the priest for a safe journey to America.

The Trip to Port

Surprisingly the first part of the journey to America—the trip to the port city—was as uncertain and in some ways as harrowing as the ocean passage. For some immigrants, leaving Poland was not easy and had to be undertaken in the utmost secrecy. For instance, Poles fleeing religious persecution, criminal indictment, or military conscription did not wish to make known their intentions to leave.

Jews living in Russian-occupied Poland, for example, had to be especially secretive. Because the czarist government restricted travel out of the country for Jews, many Jews left the country in secret. This included young men who wished to escape from compulsory military service and Jews fleeing from the growing anti-Semitism or pogroms (massacres). Sophia Belkowski was only sixteen years old when she made a midnight escape to freedom in 1912. Years later she described her journey:

We started September 12 from Poland. To cross the Russian zone we walked from the village through the forest preserve all night, to Germany someplace. There were twenty-one people and two were girls, I and one other girl. A man came with a horse and buggy—part of the way we two girls rode in the buggy, but the boys walked all the way to Germany.

Most immigrants traveled with only their most essential belongings.

When we got near the border between Russia and Germany, this older man . . . had to go see the Russians, the people who watch—what they call the borderguards. . . . We walked further. . . . There was a deep trench and they [the men] put a board over the trench—then the man put his coat over it and we walked across the Russian border in to Germany.[19]

For many immigrants the first leg of the journey to America might not be by train but rather by wagon or on foot. The day of departure was an emotional one for those leaving, as family, neighbors, or even the entire village might turn out to wish the immigrants good luck on their journey and in their new home. It was an exhilarating, yet sad time, for the farther they got from home, the more the travelers realized they were leaving behind the familiar rhythms of their former life.

Besides having to make sure that all arrangements had been properly made, immigrants had also to be watchful for dangers. Thieves and swindlers always lay in wait for unsuspecting travelers, hoping to steal their money and their tickets. Families worried about being separated from loved ones or feared that if illness should strike, someone might be prevented from making the rest of the journey.

Upon arrival at the railway station, immigrants waited to catch the trains that would carry them to their next destination. For many Poles this was the first time they had ridden the train, and many remember it as one of their most exciting experiences. Traveling alone to America, Celia Rypinski describes her first train ride:

> I went with my brother to the border of Prussia, to Germany. . . . Up to that time I never saw a train. I saw such a big train—tracks and trains— and I said "What is that?" And my brother said to me, "You're going to ride one like that, maybe a couple of hours. You'll find out what they are. They make a lot of noise and ring the bells and whistles." And I did.[20]

The journey by train could take up to several weeks before the immigrants finally reached their first destination: one of the busy port cities in Germany from which they would depart for America.

Waiting to Leave

Two German shipping lines, the North German Line out of Bremerhaven and the Hamburg American Line out of Hamburg, carried the majority of Polish emigrants to the United States. The ocean voyage itself could take as little as three weeks or as long as several months.

While waiting for their ship to depart, Polish emigrants, as well as thousands of others from eastern Europe, stayed in lodging that the steamship companies provided. In Hamburg, at the *Auswanderer-Hallen*, or "emigrant village," lived as many as four thousand travelers at any one time. Here at the company's expense, emigrants received another physical examination. They also had to answer a series of questions, similar to those to which they would have to respond when they reached Ellis Island. Steamship companies also took the time to fumigate passengers' baggage and clothing in order to remove any germs and lice present in the emigrants' belongings.

For many of the Polish emigrants, their lodging in the emigrant village was better than the homes they had left behind. In these villages many for the first time saw electric lights, took a shower, or used steam radiators. For those travelers who had a little money, the shipping company operated a clothing store in the village. To ease boredom, daily band concerts were scheduled to help pass the time while waiting for the ships.

Departure Day

The day of departure was filled with excitement and anxiety, as the Polish emigrants prepared to board the ship with others from eastern Europe, such as Russians and Czechs. The first sight of the ship was a memorable experience. Many of the ships were as long as, or longer than, the village streets; one emigrant recalled that the smokestacks of his ship reminded him of church spires. The emigrants crowded the docks, waiting for ferries to take them to the ship. The ferries made several trips back and forth between the docks and the ships. With each new group of emigrants, there was a rush up the gangplank as they scrambled to the main deck.

By law the steamship companies had to provide each adult male with 100 cubic feet of space, or roughly an area five feet wide, five feet long, and four feet high, on the upper steerage deck of the ship, and 120 cubic feet, or an area approximately five feet wide, five feet long, and five feet high on the lower steerage deck. The laws also stipulated that if a ship traveled with more than fifty passengers, it was to be equipped with an infirmary and a doctor. In addition, shipping companies were to

Farmers wave to a departing train. The train ride to one of Germany's port cities often took several weeks, and it was only the first leg of a very long journey.

A steamship leaves the docks at Hamburg. Most Polish travelers were amazed by the massive size of the ships and their smokestacks.

provide three meals a day for each passenger. Each meal was to be served at a table. The company was also ordered to provide adequate hygiene and sanitation facilities.

Daily Life in Steerage

Reality did not often match these ideal accommodations. The majority of emigrants were housed in the "steerage" areas of the ship that consisted of large holds, or rooms, located below the other decks. As many as nine hundred persons could be crowded into steerage, with bunks arranged in tiers. As a result, the emigrants had little in the way of privacy, clean quarters, or decent food.

The shipping companies expected to make the greatest profit from the passengers traveling in steerage, so the more crowded steerage was, the better for the company. Companies did as little as possible to accommodate the multitudes. They outfitted the steerage decks with only the barest essentials: iron-frame bunks, inexpensive blankets typically used for horses, and straw mattresses that soon grew lumpy and uncomfortable. For meals the company provided each steerage passenger with a cheap cup, plate, bowl, and utensils made of tin. These were of such poor quality that the dishes and utensils quickly rusted from exposure to the salty sea air and from the salt water used for cleaning them. If a passenger lost dishes or utensils, the company would not replace them.

Steerage had wooden floors. Prior to sailing, the crew swept them every morning and then sprinkled them lightly with sand to absorb moisture. During the voyage, however, the floors of the steerage quarters became filthy and were never cleaned.

Some shipping companies provided segregated areas, with the women and small children staying in one section and men residing in another. Other ships had "marriage quarters" in which families and small children could travel together. Young, single women traveling alone often stayed together in one part of the steerage quarters and tried to look after each other's welfare. Life in steerage was crowded, noisy, dirty, and sometimes unhealthy.

Edward A. Steiner, an Austrian immigrant and college professor doing research for a book, made the voyage across the Atlantic as a steerage passenger several times. In his book *On the Trail of the Immigrant*, published in 1906, Steiner writes about the horrible conditions to be found in the steerage quarters of the ships. Despite government regulations, Steiner reported that conditions on shipboard were even worse than before the laws were enacted. Describing conditions he found on the luxury liner *Kaiser Wilhelm II*, one of the many ships that carried Polish immigrants to America, Steiner wrote:

There is neither breathing space below nor deck room above, and the 900 steerage passengers . . . are pos-

itively packed like cattle, making a walk on deck when the weather is good absolutely impossible, while to breathe clean air below in rough weather, when the hatches are down, is an equal impossibility.[21]

Steiner further described the conditions he found traveling in steerage on the *Kaiser Wilhelm II*:

On the whole, the steerage of the modern ship ought to be condemned as unfit for the transportation of human beings . . . from 200 to 400 sleep in one compartment on bunks, one above the other, with little light and no comforts. . . . The unsavory rations are not served, but doled out; with less courtesy than one would find in a charity soup kitchen. The steerage ought to be and could be abolished by law. It is true that the . . . Polish peasant may not be accustomed to better things at home and might not be happier in better surroundings or know how to use them; but it is a bad introduction to our way of life to treat him like an animal when he is coming to us.[22]

Other reports compiled by immigration officials spoke of similar conditions. One immigrant official concluded that the conditions in steerage were among some of the worst living conditions ever experienced. Gradually steamship companies did away with steerage as a travel class and instead replaced it with third-class

A Treacherous Voyage

Besides seasickness, noise, bad food, and poor accommodations, immigrants traveling to America also faced other dangers. Mary Marchak, emigrating from Poland with her mother in 1913, describes a dangerous storm that their ship ran into during the voyage, in Shirley Blumenthal's Coming to America: Immigrants from Eastern Europe:

It happened about three o'clock in the morning. They say we hit an iceberg. There was an awful jar. It threw me right out of bed. And then the sailors were knocking on everybody's cabin telling them to go up, go up. We were on the bottom deck, so we had to go all the way up. The deck was just full. It was dark, foggy and you couldn't see a thing. And everybody was crying and carrying on. And I saw tears in my mother's eyes. She put a rosary in my hand and she said, "You pray honey. You pray." Everybody was hollering. And they're pulling somebody back because he was going to jump overboard. And the men were running back and forth, and getting the lifeboats and sliding them down the ropes. . . . Oh, and that noise, booing—the ship's foghorn—Boooooo! That was in my ears for the longest time. Another ship rescued us, but most of our belongings were lost on the ship that was wrecked. The only thing we still had with us was a wicker basket.

Immigrants are crowded together in the ship's steerage section.

accommodations, which, while humble, were often a vast improvement over steerage.

On Deck

Whenever weather permitted, immigrants naturally fled to the upper decks to avoid the cramped and foul conditions below. No matter if it was day or night, it was not uncommon to see many people walking about the deck taking in the clean air. All passengers tried to make the most of their time in the good weather, for at the first sign of bad weather, everyone went below deck again. One immigrant who came over in 1920 later recalled his time on deck:

> Time between meals was spent on the deck if the weather was good. Some immigrant would always come out with a harmonica or some musical instrument and the dance would follow. And during the day, of course, there were always acquaintances to be made, discussions about America, the conditions in America, and the preparation for life in America.[23]

Finally the day that so many had waited for came at last: The day the ship arrived in the United States. But the journey was not yet over. There was another ferry to take, more lines in which to wait, more crowds, and more noise. Yet somehow everything had changed. The next stop was the processing station at Ellis Island. Here Poles and other immigrants learned whether the hardship and expense of their journey had been worth the effort, for they were about to find out whether they could stay in the United States.

CHAPTER FOUR

The Golden Door to America

Perhaps one of the most awesome sights for many Polish immigrants was their first glimpse of America. Sailing into New York Harbor was for many one of the most memorable moments of their lives. For Polish immigrant Celia Rypinski, the first sight of America was the "lady with the torch," or the Statue of Liberty. She later described her first day in America:

I saw the Statue of Liberty. And we all ran out and I prayed because I heard so much in Poland about it— the Statue of Liberty. Then we pulled into the harbor and it was in the evening. We had to stay all day Sunday on the boat, until Monday morning. That was all right but we were disappointed—not only me, but everybody. Because they didn't unload on Sunday; people didn't work on Sunday.[24]

The thrill of seeing the Statue of Liberty, though, was overshadowed by the need to deal with the realities of the Ellis Island immigration station. It was here at Ellis Island that the final decision would be made as to whether the immigrants would be allowed to come into the country. For immigrants like Celia, their fear at arriving in a strange new country was also mixed with great excitement and curiosity about their new home and new lives.

Ellis Island

For the great wave of Polish immigrants who arrived in the United States during the late nineteenth century, the official port of entry was through the brand-new buildings at Ellis Island. The island itself was nothing special. Little more than a large sandbar, Ellis Island was just one of the small, flat, low islands that lie in upper New York Harbor. But on January 1, 1892, the island, which had once been the scene of public hangings during the eigh-teenth century, now had a new purpose: the processing and recording of the thousands of immigrants who streamed to America.

By 1900 the centerpiece of the 27.5-acre island facility was a large three-story, brick and white limestone-trimmed building, 400 feet in length, 165 feet wide, and over 60 feet high. Four towers marked the building corners, each of which soared 100 feet high, while three tall, arched openings spanned both the east and west sides of the building. The first floor held baggage handling facilities, railroad ticket offices, and food sales counters. But it was the second floor where the fates of the many immigrants who traveled to America rested. Known as the Great Hall, the

Transfer barges wait in front of the immigration buildings at Ellis Island. The island was the official point of entry for all immigrants to the United States.

room, which measured 200 feet by 100 feet by 56 feet high, was where immigrants were processed and registered.

Also located on the island were a hospital, a powerhouse, a surgeon's quarters, a bathhouse, and a detention center. It was estimated that, when operating at full capacity, the Ellis Island station could process between ten thousand and fifteen thousand persons a day. From 1901 to 1910, nearly 7 million immigrants passed through Ellis Island. For the majority of immigrants who came through Ellis Island, it was not just an entrance to America; it was the "Golden Door" to the land of opportunity.

The First Steps

Most of the newly arrived immigrants had little idea what lay in store for them upon their arrival in America. Few were prepared for the actual processing that would take place at Ellis Island; many more would find the experience shocking. One immigrant, upon learning that the steerage and third-class passengers were to be detained while those with first- and second-class passage were allowed to leave the ship, later commented, "There was this slight feeling among many of us that, 'Isn't it strange that here we are coming to a country where there is complete equality, but not quite so for the newly arrived immigrants?'"[25]

Before they could even leave the ship, the immigrants were first looked at by a doctor from the Public Health Service. If there appeared to be nothing wrong, the immigrants were then packed onto a small barge for the short ride to Ellis Island. One official described the boats as "not very good boats, but they were big enough to carry hundreds at a time. They were like ferries, but stronger—they were flat bottom boats."[26] These transfer barges, as they were called, could hold anywhere from a few hundred to a thousand persons. They were also uncomfortable as there were few seats and almost no protection from the elements.

For many of the immigrants the experience was another horror to be endured. The same official later stated that, "The immigrants were fearful, [and] terribly afraid."[27] Adding to their fear and uncertainty was the fact that quite often upon docking at Ellis Island the immigrants were not allowed to leave the barges right away. It was common for barges filled with people to sit for hours, waiting for those immigrants ahead of them to be processed. One immigrant who later found work at a food concession at Ellis Island remembered the ordeal:

> Sometimes when that little boat . . . came in at twelve o'clock, everybody went for dinner, doctors, and watchmen and everything. Maybe the immigrants would have to wait until two o'clock or four o'clock—they would have no chance to get into the building because it was full . . . so we fed them . . . there.[28]

On days when the barges needed to depart immediately to ferry another boatload of immigrants, the passengers could leave the boats but were ordered to stand in line

Flags adorn the Registry Hall inside the main building at Ellis Island. Immigrants often waited hours before being allowed to enter the building.

outside the main building until officials permitted them to enter. A small canopy offered some relief from the weather.

The Registry Hall

While they waited for permission to enter the main building, the immigrants were placed in groups of thirty. Sometimes after hours of waiting, immigrants were allowed to enter the building for processing. The first stop was at the ground floor baggage room where immigrants were to leave their belongings. From there, immigrants were directed to a large, dark, tiled entrance corridor and toward a flight of stairs where the Registry Hall, or the

Great Hall as it was known, was located. Here immigrants received another physical examination and were given other tests to determine whether they would be allowed to stay in America. But even while climbing the stairs and being shouted at by immigration officials, the immigrants were undergoing yet another examination by watchful members from the U.S. Public Health Service. Using what came to be known as the "six-second medical examination," these officials carefully scanned the incoming crowd, watching for individuals who had trouble climbing the stairs. Health Service officials knew that observing even the simplest of tasks could reveal a number of ailments that warranted closer examination. In 1904 a journalist posing as an immigrant wrote of his experience entering Ellis Island:

> Half-way up the stairs, an interpreter stood telling the immigrants to get their health tickets ready. . . . The majority of people, having their hands full of bags, boxes, bundles, and children carried their tickets in their teeth, and just at the head of the stairs stood a young doctor in the Marine Hospital Service uniform who took them [the tickets], looked at them, and stamped them with the Ellis Island stamp.[29]

Upon reaching the top of the stairs the immigrants entered the Registry Hall. The room was immense. The Registry Hall was further divided into a maze of passageways known as "pens." Here immigrants underwent still more examinations to determine whether their mental and physical health required treatment or, in the most severe cases, deportation. The noise and the heat from the thousands of bodies passing through the room were overwhelming, adding to the immigrants' mounting fear and bewilderment at their new surroundings.

Passing Through the Line

Upon reaching the central examining area, the immigrants were taken through the first step of a two-step medical examination from doctors with the U.S. Public Health Service. Spaced evenly apart, the immigrants moved along in a single-file line past a team of two doctors who were located some distance apart. Because on average the doctors examined as many as five thousand immigrants a day, an exam seldom lasted more than two to three minutes.

An agent inspects eyelids for signs of disease. The Registry Hall's passageways and pens are also seen here.

With an interpreter standing nearby, the doctors asked the immigrants questions about their age, general health, origins, and destination. At the same time, the doctors examined the face, neck, hands, and hair. Doctors were also careful to note how each immigrant walked, for lameness could interfere with a person's ability to hold a job. According to one observer, although the examination was quick, it was comprehensive.

The doctors were also attentive for signs of certain diseases, particularly favus, a fungal disease of the scalp; tuberculosis; and trachoma, an infection of the eyes that, if untreated, caused blindness. All three diseases are highly contagious and were, at that time, difficult to cure. These diseases, with the exception of tuberculosis, were also virtually unknown in the United States, so health officials wanted to make sure that they did not spread. Some of these examinations could be painful, especially the test for trachoma in which doctors used a buttonhook to inspect the outside and inside of a person's eyelids. Immigrants' screams of pain could be heard all the way down the line.

Catherine Bolinski remembered the medical examination well. She had come to America from Poland with a sty, or inflammation, of one eye. Although she had been treated by a doctor on the voyage over, the young woman was still worried that she would not pass the medical examination at Ellis Island. She later described her experience in an interview:

They turned your eye over—I had to blink a couple of times that way. I'll never forget it. They looked at your throat, and to see if you had any rashes on your body. I wasn't unbuttoning [my clothing] fast enough, so they shoved me out of sight. My mother got scared; she thought they were going to send me back. But then they said, "If you're unbuttoned, come on out," so I came out and was with my mother again.[30]

A Piece of Chalk

In addition to looking for signs of contagious disease, the doctors at Ellis Island relied on a special coded letter system to indicate medical problems that required further attention. Immigrants identified as having visible health problems had either the back or front of their clothing marked with chalk. This simple code identified a host of health problems. For instance, an "H" meant heart trouble, while "Ct" signified trachoma. People who were mentally ill were marked with an "X," while those who were senile had an "S" chalked onto their clothing. Pregnant women were chalked with the letters "Pg."

Those immigrants who had been marked with chalk were taken out of line and moved to another screened detention area known as the "cages," where they were visible to the other immigrants moving through the lines. Here doctors conducted more thorough medical examinations to determine whether the immigrant was healthy enough to enter the United States. Those who were thought to be too ill were removed to one of the many dormitories for observation. Others were taken to the bathhouse for a thorough treatment with disinfectant. Those with serious ailments were taken immediately to the Ellis Island hospital. Those who were given a clean bill of health were allowed to return to the main line for processing. In extreme cases, a person deemed too ill to enter the country was deported.

Family members held their breath as each person went through the physical examination. One of the immigrants' worse fears was that of being "chalked," for it meant that family members could be separated. Even worse was the realization that if family members were taken out of the line, they might not ever see each other again.

The Last Hurdles

Still in the same groups of thirty, the immigrants moved to a series of benches that separated the medical examination area from the main inspection area. As each group was called, the immigrants moved to another series of benches that were arranged in long, narrow aisles. Here they waited in single file for the next examination. While they waited, another official questioned them about their family relationships, particularly how the men and women were related to each other. This was done to identify women who might have come to America to engage in prostitution.

When a registry clerk was available, each group was called forward one at a time and told to form a straight line. Next, each person waited his or her turn to appear before the clerk to answer a series of questions. By then many of the questions

asked of the immigrants were familiar, for the representatives of the steamship companies had asked similar questions before the immigrants had departed for America.

The questions covered a variety of topics, but were essentially designed to satisfy concerns about whether persons had sufficient means to support themselves in the United States. For instance, immigrants were asked if they had family with whom they could reside and if they had any job prospects. Other questions included their names, country of origin, age, and occupation. In addition, each examiner also asked questions intended to identify individuals who might threaten the national security or pose a danger to the public.

As with the medical examinations, the clerks took about two minutes to decide whether a person was fit to stay in the United States. In addition to answering personal questions, each immigrant was also asked to do simple arithmetic exercises. Adult immigrants also had to show proof that that they had brought with them the equivalent of twenty-five American dollars. Stanley Roszak, who emigrated from German-held Poland in 1914, remembered how his father handled the officials at Ellis Island:

I thought we were sent to a concentration camp because they didn't land us in New York, but landed us on Ellis Island. There you had to sit and they called you and pushed you. There was a barricade so that you could walk in a row. You walked up, they asked you your name and they asked you this and they asked you

A Difficult Question

One of the most difficult tasks that faced new immigrants was proving to officials that they were capable of holding a job, without letting it be known that a job was waiting for them. This was because the Alien Contract Labor Law, which went into effect in 1885, denied admission to any immigrant who had signed a labor contract before arriving in America. The law was aimed at protecting the jobs of Americans from immigrants who would do the same work for less. Fiorello H. La Guardia, who served as an interpreter at Ellis Island for a short time and who would later become mayor of New York City, described the tricky situation an immigrant faced in Mary Shapiro's book Gateway to Liberty: The Story of the Statue of Liberty and Ellis Island:

It is a puzzling fact that one provision of the Immigrant Law excludes any immigrant who had no job and classifies him as likely to become a public charge [vagrant], while another provision excludes an immigrant if he has a job! Common sense suggested that any immigrant who came to the United States in those days to settle permanently surely came here to work. However, under the law, he could not have any more than a vague hope of a job. In answering the inspectors' questions, immigrants had to be very careful, because if their expectations were too enthusiastic, they might be held as coming in violation of the contract labor provision. Yet, if they were too indefinite, if they knew nobody, had no idea where they were going to get jobs, they might be excluded.

that, and they asked if you had any money so that you could take care of yourself. We said "Yes," and my father wanted to show it, but they said, "Oh, no, no, you don't have to show." They believed him; and they made a white cross on a yellow card.[31]

A New Country, a New Name

Estimates suggest that approximately 75 percent of immigrants passed through Ellis Island with little or no trouble. However, that does not mean that they were not changed by the experience. In fact, one simple question asked of them, "What is your name?" had profound consequences for a number of immigrants.

While some immigrant officials tried to be careful in spelling immigrant names, others, because they were in a rush, were not as thoughtful. Often these officials misunderstood the replies the immigrants gave, or badly misspelled the names. Still others suggested more "Americanized" names to the new immigrants. Some officials simply changed the name to make it easier to spell and pronounce.

For some immigrants, name changes posed no problem. Many saw their arrival in America as a new beginning, so a new name seemed appropriate. Tens of thousands of others, however, objected to the actions of immigration officials. Those immigrants who wanted their names to stay the same found there was little they could do. Many immigrants were too afraid to speak out, fearing that they would be branded as troublemakers and not allowed to enter the country. Other immigrants, because they were illiterate in their native languages as well as in English, had no idea what had happened until long after the deed was done. One official who witnessed these name changes take place on many occasions described what happened to many Polish immigrants: "For instance a Polish name would be Skyzertski and they [the officials] didn't even know how to spell it, so it would be changed to Sansa, to names like that. It was a much easier way."[32]

These official name changes caused problems later on when people applied for citizenship. Immigrants who did not realize that their names had been changed at Ellis Island continued to use the names they had used in Europe. As a result, their applications for citizenship were often delayed as clerks searched the records for the official names given at Ellis Island.

The "Isle of Tears"

For those who had satisfactorily answered the officials' questions, the time had come for them finally to leave Ellis Island. With their "landing cards" (a document that certified they were in America legally) in hand, these immigrants were escorted to an area on the other side of the registry desk. This section was also known by a sadder name: the "Stairs of Separation." It was here that families and friends could be divided into two groups: those who were allowed to leave and those who were to be detained or even deported. From start to finish the entire process of going through Ellis Island could take as long as two to three hours or an entire day.

While for some immigrants Ellis Island became the "Golden Door," it was also known as the "Isle of Tears" and "Hell's Island." For the millions of immigrants who were processed and allowed to leave, there were thousands who never made it past the doctors and registry clerks. Those who were ill or had no money were deported, often at the shipping company's expense. Those immigrants who were deemed physically or mentally incapable of earning a living or who were assessed to be a political or public menace were also sent home. In some instances foreign governments requested that Ellis Island officials detain and deport a runaway spouse, child, or criminal. Women traveling alone had a particularly difficult time and were often detained until immigration officials could determine whether they had family or friends in the United States who could look after them.

Through the Gate

With their experience at Ellis Island over, immigrants now had three ways to consider making their way in America. Those who intended to spend time in New York City followed a stairway that led back down to the lower level. Here they retrieved their baggage. Then, making their way down a wire-enclosed path, they waited for the ferry to take them from Ellis Island to the Battery in lower Manhattan. Here family and friends might be waiting for them. The ferry landing was then the scene of many joyous reunions.

For the majority of immigrants, however, the next destination was a large hall where they could change their money into U.S. currency and purchase train tickets to their next destination. One immigrant described this busy and loud scene:

There was a group of inspectors, young fellas only, who knew all kinds of languages. One of these young men was the leader of a bunch of immigrants. He would slip a button on you and say, "Watch me." You watched him, you followed him, and he took you to New York on the dock. From there, if you were going to Chicago or someplace, you went on another boat, a ferry to Hoboken. Then the inspector put the immigrants on the train. He knew which cars would take them. The immigrant already had the ticket and so on paid and everything. And everyone had a place or some address where they going. They stayed on the train until the conductor told them where to get off.[33]

Immigrants lug their things to a New York train station after being processed at Ellis Island. Those who were denied entry were typically deported.

Hard Conditions

Despite the best intentions to keep Ellis Island free of corrupt officials and businesses, immigration officials faced a daunting task. William Williams served as commissioner of immigration at Ellis Island from 1902 to 1905 and again from 1909 to 1914. He describes the conditions found at Ellis Island when he first took over, in Mary Shapiro's book Gateway to Liberty: The Story of the Statue of Liberty and Ellis Island:

[Immigrants] were hustled about and addressed in rough language by many of the Government and railroad officials. . . . The fact that the quarters in which they were detained were formerly called "pens" is suggestive of the rest of the treatment they received; nor can any exception be taken to the former application of this word to these quarters, in view of their filthy condition. This was particularly the case with the dining room, the floor of which was allowed by the former . . . holder to remain covered with grease, bones, and remnants of food for days at a time. . . . I witnessed with my own eyes the fact that immigrants were fed without knives, forks, or spoons. . . . The kitchen methods and methods of serving food are filthy and unsanitary in every way . . . and as the number of bowls of soup and meat are entirely insufficient in number, it is the common practice to use the same bowl over and over until all have been supplied.

There was also a fourth area, where no immigrants wished to go. In this room another immigration official sat in front of a barred gate that guarded the entrance to the detention room. Immigrants who had not satisfactorily answered officials' questions were sent here.

Detentions could vary, lasting as long as one to two days to several weeks. In general, only a comparatively small percentage of immigrants, approximately 2 percent, were ultimately prevented from entering the United States. Still, the despair that radiated from the detention area touched all who passed through Ellis Island; one female immigrant recalled that "everybody was sad there."[34]

For those who had successfully passed through the halls of Ellis Island, the journey was still not over. Now it was time to make their way and their fortunes in America and to get on with life.

CHAPTER FIVE

To Work

For almost all Polish immigrants, the first order of business upon their arrival in America was to find a job. In the late nineteenth and early twentieth centuries the United States was enjoying a period of economic expansion primarily in the cities and industrial areas, and so it was to these areas that the Polish immigrants flocked. The cities of the Midwestern and Middle Atlantic states were particularly attractive, as well as cities such as New York and Buffalo, the mining areas in Pennsylvania, and the steel manufacturing centers of Pittsburgh and Cleveland. For the most part, the settlement of the Poles was fairly centralized in that

they tended to settle in the area bounded by the Great Lakes on the north, the Mason-Dixon Line to the south, and the Missouri River to the west.

The Poles also found work in midwestern cities such as Omaha, Toledo, St. Louis, and St. Paul where slaughterhouses, refineries, and mills were located. Chicago and Detroit also attracted large numbers of Polish immigrants who sought work. In many cases friends and relatives helped newcomers. In other cases local businessmen, such as the grocer or a saloonkeeper, might recruit laborers. In time, centralized communities began to appear, particularly in Chicago

Major Polish American Communities in the United States

San Francisco

Los Angeles

Milwaukee • • Detroit • Buffalo
Chicago • • Cleveland
Baltimore • • Philadelphia

Houston •

and Buffalo. A fortunate few, at most be-tween a tenth and a fifth of the total num-ber of Polish immigrants, actually real-ized their dream of owning land. During the late nineteenth century, a number of Poles moved from cities to the country-side. Some workers also managed to save enough from their factory jobs to buy land, while others found work as farm la-borers in the hope that they, too, would eventually save enough money to buy land.

The Lure of Steady Money

Most of the immigrants who came to America from Poland were young, unmar-ried men. Often arriving alone or in groups, these newcomers struck out to make their way in America. By the time they left Ellis Island they carried, on average, only four-teen dollars in their pockets. Some might also have a piece of paper with them bear-ing the address of a friend or relative who would arrange a place to stay and, if they were lucky, a place to work.

Although many Poles wished to own land, for others the thought of agricultural labor, even on their own land, held little appeal. Poles who had come to America primarily for economic reasons were more interested in finding work that provided a steady paycheck so they would have money to send back to loved ones in Poland. As a result many Poles joined the ranks of unskilled industrial workers, fill-ing a variety of low-paying jobs in the mines, factories, foundries, and stock-yards. Estimates suggest that, although 64 percent of the Polish immigrants had worked as farm laborers in Poland, in the United States almost 90 percent of Poles found industrial jobs. Such arrangements, as one historian has pointed out, necessitated a number of difficult challenges:

[Polish immigrants] had not only jumped an ocean, they had also jumped a century—from a self-subsistent peasant economy to a capitalist job market—for this they had to pay a high price of uncertainty, of lack of security, and of homesickness.[35]

Many employers believed that the Poles worked harder than members of other ethnic groups. For instance, many factory owners were eager to hire Polish immigrants, whom they believed were best suited for heavy industrial work because of their reputation for "silent submission, their amenity to discipline, and their willingness to work long hours and overtime without a murmur."[36] Because of these widely held assumptions, many Polish workers found it difficult to move into less dangerous jobs in industries such as steel mills and factories. Despite these prejudices, Poles quickly gravitated to the steel mills of Pittsburgh and Cleveland, to the steel mills and refineries of Toledo and South Bend, and to the meat-packing plants of Omaha, Chicago, and St. Louis.

Sometimes labor recruiters, who sought newly arrived immigrants and offered them jobs, hired Poles. Yet, unlike the Italians and Greeks who relied on a patron to find them jobs, the Poles more often than not relied on each other in their search for work. In many cases a Polish worker asked his employer to hire other Poles. Some employers even asked their Polish workers to write to friends and family in Poland to find out if they wished to fill empty slots in a factory or mine. If, however, Poles applied for jobs on their own, they were often told that no jobs were available. One Polish immigrant in Pittsburgh explained, "You got a job through somebody at work who got you in. I mean this application, that's a big joke. They [management] just threw them away."[37] Alternatively, like members of other groups, Polish immigrants found that if they wanted to work, they had to pay for a job by kicking back a portion of their wages to an unscrupulous company official.

Polish immigrants also went to employment agencies, located in many large cities. These agencies often put together work crews who were sent to jobs in other parts of the country. But sometimes the agencies took advantage of the Poles who spoke little or no English and had no knowledge of their legal rights. In 1908 a social worker sent to investigate conditions among Polish immigrants described the deceitful practices in which these agencies engaged:

Men are employed for this kind of work not as individuals, but in groups of thirty or more, and are sent to parts of the country of which they are entirely ignorant. The maximum "registration fee" which employment agents may charge is fixed by statute at two dollars. . . . [But] an investigator . . .

was told frankly, "We can charge all we can get." Fees are higher when the applicant is unable to speak English.[38]

For many of the newly arrived Polish immigrants, their first jobs were as "scabs," or strikebreakers, hired to take the place of workers on strike. Employers used them as strikebreakers because they were generally excluded from union membership. Many American workers saw Poles, because of their willingness to work for low wages under dangerous conditions, as a threat to their jobs. The striking workers looked down upon Poles and did not seek them out as new union members.

Difficult Adjustments

Whenever possible, the Polish immigrants chose where and for whom they worked. In some cases Poles, like other immigrants, took or refused jobs for cultural

Destination: The West

During the mid-to-late nineteenth century, as many Poles gravitated toward the cities to look for work, a smaller number moved to the Midwest and the western regions of the United States in search of their own land and a farm that could be called home. Soon a number of Polish farming colonies appeared in Ohio, Indiana, Illinois, Michigan, Nebraska, and Texas. While many Poles started out working as farm laborers, some soon earned enough money to strike out on their own. Others got their start as small truck farmers who planted enough food to take to nearby city markets where they then sold their goods.

For those who tackled the tough land of the prairies, there were numerous challenges in starting a farm. Not only did the Polish immigrants have to deal with a strange and different environment, but they also faced other obstacles, such as grasshopper plagues, dry summers, and harsh winters. Because there was a shortage of animals used for plowing and harvesting, breaking up the tough prairie soil was particularly difficult.

Despite these difficult beginnings, the Polish immigrant farmers made the most of their lot. They learned to rely on the available wild game for meat and in time learned to grow what they called "Turkish wheat," or corn, one of the few crops that flourished in the prairie. They also learned that in order to survive they needed to grow crops that would do well in their new land, rather than trying to grow the same kinds of food that they had grown in Poland. But for many Poles, owning a farm was too difficult. Also, throughout the late nineteenth century, land prices increased, and with the additional cost of running a farm, the venture was simply too expensive for the majority of Poles who came to America.

reasons. Men from Russian Poland and those from Galicia, for example, would not accept positions as needleworkers, believing those jobs were "women's work." In fact the dirtiest and most dangerous jobs drew Polish immigrants. The less desirable the job was, the greater the opportunity for making money.

Taking mining and steelworking jobs meant making adjustments. For many Poles used to working in the fields, toiling for hours underneath the earth or in a searing hot mill was a difficult change. Working outside meant following the natural rhythms of the day and the seasons. But working in a factory meant adjusting to the clock. The work was not seasonal, as was farmwork, and it was hard, dirty, and often unhealthy labor, six days a week, twelve months a year.

Even when a Pole found a job, he often learned that the wages were low. The New York Mills Corporation, located in central New York, hired many Poles as weavers. They worked at special machines spinning cloth. Weavers earned on average between $6 and $9 for a fifty-six-hour work week. For every defective thread found, whether it was the worker's fault or not, the owner deducted twenty-five cents from the worker's paycheck. Adding to workers' troubles was a system in which a worker wishing to work in another position had to have secured written permission from his or her foreman. Since permission was unlikely to be given because of the prejudice against Polish workers, it was almost impossible for a worker to get ahead. Still, many Polish immigrants recognized that their lot in life had changed. As one Pole

A young Polish boy takes a break from spinning cloth.

wrote in a letter home, "I have work, I'm not hungry, only I have not yet laughed since I came to America."[39]

Steel workers also received low wages. In 1902 Poles employed at the Lackawanna Steel Company earned an average of $1.50 a day. When the company suffered an economic slowdown, workers' wages dropped to $1.38. In 1911 the average American family of four needed $560 a year to live. Workers at the Lackawanna plant earned only $502 a year for working twelve hours a day, six days a week.

The Foreman

No matter what the job, Polish immigrants were always at the mercy of the foreman, or supervisor. The foreman decided who worked each job, set work rules, and maintained discipline. More important, the foreman hired and fired the workers. Usually the foremen were members of another immigrant group, such as German or Irish, who had little liking for the newcomers.

In many cases the foreman's authority was undisputed, reminding many Polish immigrants of their powerful landlords in the old country. Polish workers found themselves the targets of both physical and mental abuse. The foremen also thought nothing of demanding special favors or of underpaying a worker. The foreman's power was so great that Polish immigrants could do little to oppose him if they wanted to keep on working.

Many Polish immigrants were no doubt disappointed and frustrated at the conditions under which they had to work. Some Poles became bitter and wrote angry letters home describing their lives in America. An anonymous Polish immigrant asserted:

> What people from America write to Poland is all bluster; there is not a word of truth. For in America Poles work like cattle. Where a dog does not want to sit, there the Pole is made to sit, and the poor wretch works because he wants to eat.[40]

Dangerous Work

Yet Poles did indeed want to eat; it was hunger that had driven many of them to leave their homeland. Thus Poles willingly took jobs in damp and gaseous mines, always aware that at any moment a mineshaft might collapse. In the ironworks Poles worked as foundrymen, where in sweltering heat they breathed the toxic fumes of the molten metals they poured into a smoking crucible. Polish immigrants also worked as still-cleaners in oil refineries, where they chipped out "coke," a soft kind of coal, inside 250-degree refining stills. The heat and grime in these jobs were so intense that one doctor commented that the Polish workers looked like "boiled meat."[41] A journalist visiting one of the Carnegie Steel Company's plants in Homestead, Pennsylvania, in 1892, described the horrific conditions he found inside the factory:

> Everywhere in the enormous sheds were pits gaping like the mouth of hell, and ovens emitting a terrible degree of heat, with grimy men filling and lining them. One man jumps down, works desperately for a few minutes, and is then pulled up, exhausted. Another immediately takes his place; there is no hesitation.[42]

Working conditions in the textile mills were not much better. The noise was deafening from the constant clatter of the mechanical shuttle looms moving back and forth. One worker remembered that "the people who worked in the weave shop had their own language. It was a hand or sign language. You learned lip reading."[43] Some workers tried stuffing their ears with the lint they had scraped from the equipment. In general, people

No Child's Play

Young Polish immigrant boys grew up fast when they came to America. As soon as they were able, they were sent out to work, as their families needed every penny they could get in order to survive. Some Polish boys as young as nine went to work in the mines where they began working as "breakers." A social reformer who visited a mine in Pennsylvania in 1906 describes the working conditions of the "breaker" boys. The description appears in Shirley Blumenthal's book Coming to America: Immigrants from Eastern Europe:

Work in the coal breakers is exceedingly hard and dangerous. Crouched over the chutes, the boys sit hour after hour picking out the pieces of slate and other refuse from the coal as it rushes past to the washers. From the cramped position they have to assume, most of them become more or less deformed and bent-backed like old men. . . . The coal is hard, and accidents to the hands, such as cut, broken, or crushed fingers are a worse accident; a terrified shriek is heard, and a boy is mangled and torn in the machinery, or disappears in the chute to be picked out later smothered and dead. Clouds of dust fill the breakers and are inhaled by the boys, laying the foundation for asthma and miner's consumption [black lung disease.]

could tell who worked as a weaver because they were so hard of hearing. One Polish worker describing his workplace wrote, "Here you hear only noise, thousands of people going here and there, and the factory whistles. Yes they have birds and flowers, but they are far away."[44]

Besides the noise, weavers were also exposed to continual dampness because the fibers needed to be moist. The dampness of the work area, in addition to the dust and lint that was always present in the air, led to numerous ailments of the throat, lungs, and respiratory system. Workers often came down with cases of chronic laryngitis, or worse. Tuberculosis, a deadly infectious disease that attacks the lungs, also claimed the lives of many Polish textile workers.

Like miners and steel or foundry workers, the Poles who worked in the textile factories had to be careful around the equipment. The shuttles used to loom the cloth were heavy pieces of equipment with seventeen-inch wooden pieces topped by metal tips. Occasionally these tips would loosen and fly off the shuttle with great force. Those workers caught in the tip's path, if lucky, escaped with only cuts and bruises. Those less fortunate lost their eyes, limbs, and sometimes their lives.

Adding to the dangerous environment in factories was the lack of helpful safety information. Safety information that was available, such as warning signs, were printed only in English. As a result, workers who did not speak English had the highest incidence of work-related accidents. Because few foremen spoke the language of their workers, there was little the Polish workers could do except to be as careful as possible. Their caution was not always enough to protect them from serious injury or death.

Foundry workers fill molds with hot, molten steel. Many Polish immigrants worked in jobs as dangerous as this one.

A Growing Labor Force

Labor unions initially resisted adding immigrants to their membership, but attitudes changed by the late nineteenth century. Some unions, such as the United Mine Workers in 1897, appealed to Polish-born workers to join. These efforts paid off. By 1902, as membership swelled, the union won significant concessions from mining companies. The United Textile Workers also hired Polish labor organizers to attract Polish workers and printed much of their union materials in Polish. This created an increase in Polish membership.

Organizing Polish workers, however, was not easy, in part due to language barriers and cultural differences. By the first decade of the twentieth century, union leaders employed Polish-speaking members as organizers and began to hold meetings in Polish neighborhoods. They also met with Polish church leaders and advertised in the Polish-language newspapers.

In the fight for better working conditions and higher pay, Polish workers often found themselves in the line of fire. In May 1886 a labor dispute in Milwaukee resulted in what was called a "riot," in which five persons, all of them Polish immigrant workers, were killed. One of the most notorious labor disputes occurred in 1897 during a coal miners' strike in Lattimer, Pennsylvania. On September 10 the local sheriff and eighty-six deputies stopped four hundred striking miners, many of them Polish. Without warning, some of the deputies opened fired on the crowd, killing nineteen miners and wounding thirty-eight others. Known as

the "Lattimer Massacre," the event stirred members of the Polish community. As one labor historian explains:

> Those feeling the sting of the Lattimer bullets were members of the Eastern European immigrant society. Living in a strange new country, they felt the despair of being isolated, the frustration of being powerless, and the pain of exploitation. Attracted to a nation that inspired hope, they suddenly faced a situation in which members of their own group were, in their eyes, mercilessly killed and injured by a sheriff's posse without any justification. . . . [There was] the opinion that if the strikers . . . were of the English-speaking class there would have been no bloodshed.[45]

Despite these setbacks, Polish workers continued to make inroads in the labor unions. By 1900 Polish workers dominated the oil refining industry in Bayonne, New Jersey. In 1915 and again in 1916, their union successfully won concessions from Standard Oil, which resulted in pay increases and paid benefits in case a worker was ill, injured, or died on the job.

Polish Women Workers

Some Polish immigrant women also went to work. Employment opportunities for them, however, were fewer than for men, as many employers tended to prefer Polish male laborers. The majority of Polish women who worked were unmarried. Once married, Polish immigrant women

A copper miner pushes a car through the mine's dark shafts. Mining and other low-paying industrial jobs were common employment for newly arrived Poles.

left their jobs to concentrate on keeping their home and raising a family. In some cases married or widowed women might take in boarders who paid for room, meals, and laundry service. Because these tasks were done in the home and were considered traditional women's work, other Polish immigrants accepted a woman making money in this way.

Beyond running boardinghouses, the work available for women tended to be in domestic service or in light manufacturing in the textile mills and other factories. In St. Louis, Polish women toiled in nut and tobacco factories where they spent ten-hour days picking kernels out of the crushed shells. They sliced tobacco leaves in cigar makers' dusty, dark rooms. They worked as seamstresses doing piecework for garment companies in New York City and Boston, earning anywhere from 60¢ to a $1.10 for every dozen garments they completed. They scrubbed floors and washed dishes or worked as farm laborers during the harvest season. In tin can factories, they worked at equipment that could scar their faces or sever their fingers and hands.

Trzymanie Bortników

For single Polish men in search of housing, there was always *trzymanie bortników*, or "boarder-keeping." This allowed single men to live with a family for $2 to $3 a month. This included laundry, but boarders either ate out or paid extra to take their meals with the family. In areas such as mining towns, where there were few families, men would often rent a room together, with one man acting as housekeeper and cook for the others. In an effort to save money, it was common for as many as a dozen men to share one small room or a two-room apartment. In many cases a young man would continue to stay on as a boarder or with a group of men until he was ready to get married. Polish American women who took in boarders also benefited. A woman might take in anywhere from $20 to $25 a month from her boarders, which was far more than she might make at a factory or domestic job. Poles also had a higher percentage of households who took in boarders: Approximately 48.4 percent of Polish households had at least one boarder as compared with other ethnic groups, which averaged about 32.9 percent.

Finding a Place to Fit

Between 1900 and 1919, Polish immigrant workers started or joined most of the major labor strikes that marked this era of general labor unrest. With each victory, no matter how small, Polish workers gradually won the right to work for better wages and under safer working conditions. Unfortunately many Poles came to the uncomfortable realization that even though they lived and worked in America, they were still not considered Americans.

For some, life in America proved too hard. One immigrant woman wrote of her early impressions of America:

I looked about the narrow streets of squeezed-in stores and houses, ragged clothes, dirty bedding oozing out of the windows, ash-cans and garbage-cans cluttering the sidewalks. . . . "Where are the green fields and open spaces in America?" cried my heart. "Where is the golden country of my dreams?"[46]

Other Poles were not as disappointed. One young immigrant concluded that "In America you will spill more sweat in one day than in a week back home. . . . But I will not go back if someone was to give me the master's estate. . . . Once you have tasted America, there is no way back to those old miseries."[47] Like this young man, most Polish immigrants tried to become Americans and to enter the mainstream of American life, while not completely losing touch with their heritage.

CHAPTER SIX

Polonia

"We are lonely here,"[48] wrote one Polish immigrant in a letter home. As a group, Poles were slow to assimilate into American society. Their traditional clothing and the Polish language itself were too foreign and strange for many Americans. In some cases the Poles appeared physically different from Americans. This was due in part to their historical roots as descendants of the Slavic peoples who originated in eastern Europe. Because of many Americans' difficulty in accepting Poles and because of the Poles' own reluctance to enter a society they found to be both frightening and different, the establishment of Polish immigrant communities was particularly important. Here they could find the same kinds of institutions and people they were used to at home.

Still, many Polish immigrant communities were often in a state of continual change. During the early years of the twentieth century, from 40 to 60 percent of those who settled in Polish neighborhoods and communities left within ten years' time. Some went back to Poland, while others searched for a better place to live or work. Whatever the reason, the Polish immigrant communities were not as stable or traditional as many would have liked, but Polish immigrants worked hard to create a sense of place and belonging that offered a welcome refuge from the uncertainties of American life.

Polonia

The most extensive Polish communities emerged in the large cities of the Midwest and Northeast, such as Buffalo, Cleveland, Detroit, and Chicago. These and other Polish communities were often dubbed *Polonia*, the Latin name for Poland. Over time the term would also refer to the Polish American community at large. While each community might vary in size, they all had similar institutions and businesses.

Found within each were various associations and societies, small businesses, a Roman Catholic church, and the Polish-language press to maintain Polish customs and culture. Yet these communities did not re-create Poland, for in making a life for themselves the immigrants also drew on influences from their new homeland.

Among the mainstays of every Polish immigrant community were the small businesses that flourished in these neighborhoods. Comparatively few Poles pursued opportunities to own their own businesses in America; by 1920 only 1.7 percent of Polish-speaking immigrants were in business for themselves as opposed to 5.2 percent of Italians and 59.7 percent of

Today, Polish-language signs abound on Chicago's Michigan Avenue. Chicago is home to one of the country's largest Polish American communities.

Jewish immigrants from all countries. But those who did open their own businesses created some of the more stable and enduring institutions in Polonia.

Those Poles who went into business for themselves engaged in certain trades and stayed away from others. Unlike Greeks and Italians who opened up restaurants, Polish families tended to eat at home and rarely dined out, although Polish men sometimes ate meals at a neighborhood tavern, which was also a place where men could meet, talk, and relax. As a consequence there were few Polish restaurants. Polish immigrants also did not have much excess capital and so they often avoided businesses that required a large sum of money to start, such as furniture or clothing stores.

New World Business Enterprises

Poles instead operated small artisan or retail shops, such as bakeries, butcher shops, and saloons. Other Poles established businesses that catered directly to the Polish community, such as print shops or stores that carried religious merchandise. One business opportunity that proved especially successful was opening a Polish funeral parlor. Unheard of in their homeland, where making money from burying the dead was forbidden, Poles in the United States made a good living as undertakers serving the immigrant community. In time many funeral directors rose to middle-class status and gained positions of leadership among their fellow immigrants.

The majority of businesses in the Polish community, however, remained small and family owned. Many businessmen worked out of the front room in the family home and lived in the back. Frequently, the owner or his wife had other jobs besides running the business to make ends meet.

The Polish Press

One of the most important institutions in Polonia was the Polish-language press. Immigrants shared a widespread belief that these newspapers were expert on almost any subject. In any Polish-language newspaper, immigrants, if they were literate, could read local news as well as news from Poland. The newspapers also carried important information about American customs and laws and outlined the procedure immigrants needed to follow to become American citizens. The impact of these newspapers was far-reaching; they were, as one historian of Polish American life described them, the agents of "education and change."[49] For those immigrants still struggling to master English and adapt to American life, the newspapers provided comfort and a sense of the familiar, helping them to make their way in their new homeland.

The Polish press began to flourish during the 1870s. By 1893 a survey found that 105 different Polish-language newspapers and magazines had been published since 1863, the year in which the first Polish newspaper appeared in the United States. Of that number, half were still in print thirty years later, at the time the survey was conducted. A historian who has studied the Polish-language press explained why these newspapers endured:

Polish Cultural Clubs

Besides fraternal organizations and other associations and the rise of the Polish press, there were also a number of Polish cultural organizations that helped in preserving the Polish heritage. In Chicago in 1926 the first Polish Arts Club met. In Buffalo, New York, the Joseph Conrad Literary Club, named for the famous Polish author, born Józef Teodor Konrad Korzeniowski, was established. In Chicago the Polish Museum of America was created in 1935 and is still open today. Two years later, in October 1937, New York City held its first Pulaski Day Parade on Fifth Avenue, in honor of the Revolutionary War hero. Even though all these activities were created to help keep Polish culture alive, they also demonstrated how Poles were being assimilated into the American mainstream. For instance, the Conrad Literary Club conducted its business in English, and the Polish Museum chose as its focus the experience of Poles in America. Even the Pulaski parade celebrates an American event and the role a Polish hero played in it.

A well-known literary club in New York is named after Polish-born author Joseph Conrad.

The immigrant press of the later period dealt with adaptation problems, served the community interests, and were determined to operate on a sound financial basis. In order to reach the farmer and the factory worker, it had to lower the literary [standard] and tailor the content to its readers' needs and likings. Although most of the papers were typographically poorly outfitted and some lacked even the . . . markings of the Polish alphabet, they did more than their share to educate the often illiterate masses and promote their ethnic and religious self-consciousness.[50]

In Polonia there was a newspaper for everyone. Among the most influential of the Polish newspapers was *Gazeta Polska*, or *Polish Gazette*, published in Chicago. *Zgoda* (*Harmony*) and *Naród Polski* (*Polish Nation*) spoke for the Polish National Alliance and the Polish Roman Catholic Union. The Polish Roman Catholic Church also had its own newspapers such as *Polak w Ameryce* (*Pole in America*), published in Buffalo, New York. *Orzel Polski* (*Polish Eagle*) was published in Missouri, and the highly influential *Gazeta Polska Katolicka* (*Polish Catholic Gazette*) came from Detroit. Beginning in 1910 Polish women had their own newpaper, *Glos Polek* (*Polish Women's Voice*), published by the Polish Women's Alliance.

In 1888 the first Polish-language daily newspaper appeared, *Kuryer Polski* (*Polish Courier*), founded in Milwaukee. Two of the most popular dailies came from Chicago and Detroit: *Dziennik Chicagoski* (*Chicago Daily News*) and *Dziennik Polski* (*Polish Daily News*). All of these newspapers had subscribers from across the country. These were soon followed by the first English-language Polish newspaper, *The Polish American Journal*, which also established a nationwide circulation among Polish Americans.

Associations and Organizations

In the United States, as in Poland, Poles pooled their resources to provide services for the community. Organizations provided death benefits, which helped defray the cost of funerals and provided for widows, children, and orphans. Some associ-

Real Estate Boom

One strong cultural value that continued when Poles reached America was the relationship between status and land. In America this was best characterized by home ownership and the buying of land whenever possible. Despite the fact that many Poles labored in working-class jobs, many, through careful saving, were soon able to purchase their own homes. By 1887, during the first wave of Polish immigration, Poles had amassed almost $10 million worth of real property. By 1901 about one-third of the Polish immigrant community in the United States owned real estate worth an estimated $600 million. A survey done in 1930 found that in Milwaukee, 70 percent of the Poles owned their homes, compared to 33 percent of the English and Irish Americans. A similar survey done in Pennsylvania found that 57 percent of Poles were home owners compared to 23 percent of American-born whites. Whenever possible, Polish immigrants accepted an opportunity to buy more real estate.

ations offered a building and loan service. Each member contributed anywhere from fifty cents to a dollar a week to be held by the association as a down payment toward a home. Not only did the member have a down payment when he needed it, but the association often provided low-interest loans to help with the mortgage. By 1900 Polish building and loan societies in the United States held assets totaling approximately $1 million.

People who had lived in the same village or area in Poland often formed associations with one another in the United States. Yet, by the late nineteenth century, two groups in Chicago, which had one of the largest concentrations of Polish immigrants in the country, expanded to become national in scope, hoping to draw membership from Polish immigrants throughout the United States.

The effort to grow sparked a serious debate among members of the two groups. Some members considered themselves nationalists, believing that all Poles living in the United States ought to join a central association and ought to concentrate on helping to establish a free and independent Poland. Others thought that to be a Pole also meant to be a Roman Catholic. As a result they refused to admit Poles who were socialists, Jews, or atheists into the national organization.

As a result of this division Polish immigrants failed to launch a unified national organization. The two Chicago groups remained separate, each one supported by a number of smaller local and regional organizations. One of these groups, established in 1873, was the *Zjed-noczenie Polski Rzymsko-Katolickie*, the Polish Roman Catholic Union (PRCU). This organization was open to all Poles who were in good standing with the Roman Catholic Church. It was dominated by priests. The second group was the *Zwiazek Narodowy Polski*, or the Polish National Alliance (PNA), established in 1880. This group drew its support primarily from the middle class and welcomed any Pole who supported a free and independent Poland.

For both groups the hottest debate was over who constituted a true Pole. Both groups were nationalist in outlook; that is, both supported a free and independent Poland. The PNA promoted assimilation into American culture and society, while the PRCU wished to strengthen the influence of the Roman Catholic Church in Polish American communities and remain more aloof from American life. Both groups published their own newspapers, which only fueled the bitter rivalry that had developed between them and divided the immigrant community.

The constant quarreling between the two groups prompted many immigrant Poles to withdraw their support from both organizations and start new associations. Among these were the Polish National Union, founded in 1889, the Polish Union of the United States, and the Polish National Alliance of Brooklyn that emerged in 1903.

Polish immigrant women had their own organizations and clubs. In 1898 several women's groups banded together to create the *Zwiazek Polek w Ameryce*, the Polish Women's Alliance of America (PWA).

This group worked closely with the international peace movement to restore a free and independent Poland. The PWA also emphasized the "emancipation, education, and protection of women [which] would strengthen the nation and preserve Polishness through the influence of women upon the family."[51] To this end, the organization campaigned for temperance, progressive social causes, and women's political rights. By 1925 the PWA had its own newspaper and boasted a membership of twenty-five thousand. As a result of the PWA's influence the PRCU and the PNA opened their membership to women as well.

The Parish

At the center of every Polish immigrant community was the parish church. As new Polish communities formed, one of the first things done was to find a place where they could hold religious services. It was not uncommon then for Poles to gather in the back rooms of businesses or vacant buildings in order to meet and take part in religious rituals. When the number of Polish families in a neighborhood grew large enough, local leaders formed fund-raising committees in order to build a new church for the community.

Not only did the church take care of the Poles' religious and spiritual needs, it also

A church towers over a Polish American parish. The church serves as the spiritual and social center for all Polish American communities.

served as a social center where immigrants could meet and talk, and as a clearinghouse for information. Whenever an immigrant faced a problem, he or she almost invariably turned to the parish priest. By 1900 approximately 517 parishes had been established in the United States by Polish immigrants.

More than any other cultural institution that the Poles brought to America, the Catholic Church was the strongest link to their homeland. The Catholic Church in the United States maintained its extreme conservatism. Reinforcing that basic conservative view was the practice of "importing" priests and nuns from Poland. Not only did Polish immigrants want their own Polish-speaking clergy, they preferred not to attend other ethnic Catholic churches, such as those run by the Germans, Irish, or Italians, which seemed to them to be as foreign as were the Protestant churches that dominated mainstream American religious culture.

While these Polish men stuffed sausages, their wives ran the family household.

The spiritual leaders of the Polish Catholic community were the priests, who wielded social and political, as well as spiritual, power—so much so, that many immigrants called them "priest-titans." In the beginning, because the priests were often a little better educated, many immigrants felt more comfortable having the guidance of a priest. Over time, however, a battle of wills arose between parishioners and priests. At stake was determining whether the people or the clergy were better qualified to direct community affairs. As Poles took a more active role not only in their community but outside of it, they felt they were better able to handle community affairs. Others, though, because of their obedience to the church, continued to seek out their priests for guidance and advice.

Family Life

Family life in the Polish immigrant community was defined by strong patriarchal

Immigrant Polish families worked very hard, and children often labored with their parents on farms or in factories.

(fatherly) control over the family, particularly over wives and unmarried daughters. An important difference between the lives of Polish women in Poland and those living in America was that immigrant women often controlled many of the day-to-day decisions in the household. Men worked away from home, in factories and mines, rather than in the fields of the family farm. They were often unavailable for consultation when decisions had to be made. The responsibility, therefore, increasingly fell to women. While men were still regarded as the head of the family and would have the final say in major decisions, the wife had a stronger voice than before.

Life was hard for Polish immigrant women. Not only did they have to run the household, but many also helped support the family by doing laundry or sewing. Adding to their burdens was caring for their large families. Polish immigrant women routinely bore between five and ten children. They commonly gave birth without the benefit of medical care and in unsanitary conditions. Nor did women have much time to recuperate from pregnancy and childbirth. Many were back at work, cooking, cleaning, and nursing, the day after giving birth to a child.

Even in the United States the family remained at the center of private life for Poles. No one ventured far from home. Fathers tried to find work in or near the neighborhood where they lived. The male members of immigrant families, and on rare occasions some of the female members as well, found work in the same shop, factory, or mine. In some cases entire families worked together as farm laborers or oyster shuckers. Immigrant families pulled together because they needed contributions from every member to survive. Children learned at a tender age that work and family came before their individual desires and aspirations.

Families pulled together because quite often every pair of hands was needed to help pay the bills, provide food, and keep a roof over their heads. Workdays were long for everyone, often starting before sunup and going well into the night. This was particularly true for women who after the workday was through still needed to take care of home and family matters. There was little leisure time for anyone.

To help ends meet, families often took in boarders who paid $2.50 to $3 weekly for their lodging. This practice helped many Polish families. For example, in 1900 more than half of the Polish American families living in Johnstown, Pennsylvania, took in boarders, with five boarders being the average number in these residences.

Many homes in Polonia resembled the homes and farms of Poland. Each residence almost always had a vegetable garden of some sort; and it was not unusual to see animals such as cows, goats, or chickens roaming about, much to the dismay of non-Polish neighbors.

This Polish sign reads, "God Bless Our Home." Polish Americans almost always spent some of their salaries on church donations and religious objects.

The *Sokół Polski*

One of the more enduring fraternal organizations established by Polish Americans was the *Sokół Polski*, the Polish Falcon movement. Founded in 1887, the Union of Polish Falcons was created as an athletic and patriotic society, similar to that of the American YMCA. Considered to be one of the most nationalistic and patriotic organizations among the Poles, the Polish Falcons advocated the reunification of Poland with a special twist. Among the many programs that the organization sponsored were military training and physical fitness. The Falcons wished to form a separate Polish army to fight for Poland during World War I. While their goals were never completely attained, the Polish Falcons live on today with a membership of thirty-one thousand, organized into 143 groups, or "nests," as they are known. The society continues to promote educational and athletic events and also sponsors a scholarship fund for those majoring in physical education.

Poles were by nature frugal in their handling of money. Many families carefully saved every available dollar they could. When possible, the savings were spent to buy a home. Over time, additional monies were spent to acquire more land or real estate. A certain portion of a Pole's earnings was also given to the church and, when possible, to purchase a religious artifact to be placed in a special area of the home.

A Childhood Cut Short

When necessary, children, especially those of the first generation Polish immigrants, went to work. However, parents made sure that the job was suitable for the child and that it was fairly close to home. Single women might work as domestics or launderers in private homes or at restaurants and hotels. Such jobs were considered women's work, and would prepare the young woman for taking care of her own family when the time came for her to marry. If they were not already working by the time they reached the age of twelve or thirteen, children were expected to begin contributing to the family income. One Polish immigrant woman explained why children willingly helped:

> You took care of one another. You never questioned it. In our family we never expected anything in return. It was the honor that we had. The trust—that's why we felt so close to one another. There was no house divided here.[52]

As a matter of course, working children turned over their wages to their parents. In many households the parents gave back a few cents to the child for candy or entertainment. In time the need for children to contribute to the family income decreased; by 1920 only 10 percent of Polish households required children to work.

Education

The need for children to work reflected on the state of education in Polonia. For most Polish immigrants education was minimal, though many parishes allocated funds to build schools in which children received Roman Catholic instruction. Moreover, despite the growing number of Catholic schools, Polish American children rarely went beyond the eighth grade. This was due in part to the need of many Polish families to have their children work as soon as possible.

Still, over time Poles realized the importance of a Catholic education within their communities. By 1911 there were three hundred parochial (Catholic) schools in Polish American communities in the United States. By 1945 the number had doubled. In that same year fifteen thousand Polish American students were attending parochial high schools and Catholic colleges. Most Polish parents preferred sending their children to parochial rather than to public schools, believing that the public schools were unchristian and would rob their children of their heritage and their faith.

Yet there were problems with the parochial schools. Catholic schools emphasized religious instruction and neglected other subjects. The schools were also overcrowded, and in general the quality of teaching was poorer than in public schools. Students and parents in Polonia who wished to have more than a high school diploma often found themselves the targets of resentment in the community. One historian noted that "members of Polonia feel bitter towards their educated class, resent its attitude and consider it ungrateful."[53] This attitude arose in part because of Polish families needing extra income from their working children and in part from the idea that those with more education considered themselves better than the majority of working-class Poles. But over time, as more and more Polish Americans gravitated towards other American institutions in order to become more "American," attendance began dropping at the Polish parochial schools.

For Polish immigrants the need to maintain ties to their homeland helped them adjust to America. These different institutions, all in their own way, helped Polish immigrants remember their culture and heritage. This became especially important as Poles found themselves at odds with an American society that wanted little to do with them and their ways.

CHAPTER SEVEN

Trying to Fit In

Polish immigrants were pulled in two different directions. Their desire to maintain ties to Poland and to preserve their culture and heritage was very strong. At the same time, they recognized the need to adjust to life in their new home among a people that wanted little to do with them or their ways.

Like many other immigrant groups, the Poles suffered discrimination and reprisals from old-stock Americans, as well as from members of immigrant groups who had come to the United States earlier. To many Americans the Polish peasants who came to America during the first wave were dirty and ignorant. To American workers it was bad enough that Polish immigrants were willing to work low-paying jobs; even worse, the Poles braved picket lines to go to work during periods of labor unrest, threatening striking workers' job security. Some Americans were alarmed with Polish immigrants who were drawn to radical political beliefs such as socialism, which many believed made the Poles dangerous enemies not only to national security but to the American way of life. Poles who were not quick to learn English were regarded as stupid. To overcome these negative stereotypes, Poles worked very hard at becoming model Americans. These efforts, however, were not always acknowledged.

"Human Flotsam"

With the outbreak of the First World War in 1914, Americans regarded everyone who spoke English with a European accent with suspicion and fear. For years a movement known as "nativism" had been gaining momentum. The war gave it added support. Nativists believed that too many immigrants had been allowed to come into the country, particularly from southern and eastern Europe. Immigrants from these regions looked different from those of Anglo-Saxon stock, spoke incomprehensible languages, had unpronounceable names, practiced different ways of worship, and were attracted to socialism and other anti-American political creeds. That approximately 75 percent of the immigrants who came to America between 1901 and 1910 were from southern and eastern Europe was reason enough for nativists to demand that immigration be severely curtailed if not entirely prohibited. Some feared that if the government did not act, these newcomers would overrun and ruin the country.

Many high-ranking government officials shared nativist concerns, believing that the United States had let in too many "undesirable aliens." As early as 1896, nearly two decades before the start of the First World War, Senator Henry Cabot

An 1891 cartoon reveals the negative opinion most Americans held of immigrants. The man closest to the stage is labeled a "Polish vagabond."

THE EVILS OF UNRESTRICTED IMMIGRATION.

From Judge.]   [March 28, 1891.

Lodge of Massachusetts offered a gloomy forecast:

> There is an appalling danger to the American wage earner from the flood of low, unskilled, ignorant, foreign labor which has poured into the country for some years past, and which not only takes lower wages, but accepts a standard of life and living so low that the American workingman cannot compete with it.[54]

To explain their dislike of certain "foreign elements," nativists embraced a number of racial theories, supposedly based on scientific analysis, that emphasized the superiority of the Anglo-Saxon people over those from eastern and southern Europe. One of these studies went so far as to label the "new" immigrants, including the Poles, as "noisome and repulsive" and "beaten members of beaten breeds."[55] One study done in 1916, in offering a "theory" about the current crop of immigrants, also reflects the bigotry of the nativist movement:

> The new immigration . . . contained a large and increasing number of the weak, the broken and the mentally crippled of all races drawn from the lowest stratum of the Mediterranean basin and the Balkans, together with the hordes of the wretched submerged populations of the Polish Ghettos. Our jails, insane asylums and almshouses are filled with this human flotsam and the whole tone of American life . . . has been lowered and vulgarized by them.[56]

A New Quota

In an attempt to stem the growing tide of "undesirables," the U.S. government enacted a series of laws designed to decrease the number of immigrants from

The literacy test for immigrants barred many from entering the United States.

eastern and southern Europe. By the time of the first great wave of Polish immigrants, several of these laws were already in effect. For instance, as early as 1875, the government passed a law banning prostitutes and convicts from entering the United States and would automatically deport these individuals back to their homeland. In 1885 Congress enacted additional legislation to keep out the mentally ill and those whose political beliefs might lead them to foment revolution or overthrow the government. In 1896 Congress enacted a law establishing a literacy test, which all immigrants had to pass as a condition of entry into the United States. In the words of Senator Henry Cabot Lodge, the act was designed to "bear most heavily upon the Italians, Russians, [and] Poles [which are] the races most affected by the illiteracy test . . . who are most alien to the great body of the people of the United States."[57] Even Woodrow Wilson, who was president of Princeton University, governor of New Jersey, and eventually president of the United States, had little use for the Poles, describing them as coming from the "ranks where there was neither skill nor energy nor any initiative of quick intelligence."[58]

Mere criticism of the "new immigrants" did not satisfy nativist Americans. If these people were so alien to the American way of life, then perhaps the government ought to prevent all of them from coming to the United States. By the 1920s the government complied. After the First World War, anti-German feeling was high, but general antiforeign sentiments were especially powerful in the United States. In this atmosphere Congress passed a series of the most stringent and restrictive immigration laws in American history.

These new laws used a complicated quota system to limit how many immigrants from a particular foreign country would be permitted to enter the United States each year. Once a country's annual quota had been met, no more immigrants from that country would be considered for admission until the following year. The laws hit the Poles particularly hard. In 1921, before the new crackdown went into effect, 95,000 Poles immigrated to the United States. Within five years that number dropped to only 5,341. As one Polish-language newspaper bitterly complained: "This unfair system of restriction favors the recent enemies of the United States [the Germans] and discriminates against such patriotic minority groups as, for example, the Poles."[59]

Some Americans took a more generous attitude toward immigrants. They did not share the belief that immigrants could never become good Americans. Rather, they wanted to determine how best to help Poles and others enter the American mainstream; that is, to shed their identity as Polish citizens and become American citizens. Social and government agencies tried to help Poles and other immigrants to become "Americanized" through classes at the YMCA, public school programs that taught citizenship, and patriotic get-togethers. These activities encouraged immigrants to learn to speak English and to adopt American customs and culture.

A Hard Road

Almost from the beginning, however, Americans discriminated against and abused Poles. Many Poles suffered indignities of all kinds on a daily basis. In stores, they were pushed around and made fun of while they tried to shop. Americans laughed at their clothing and heavy boots and mocked their halting and broken English. Shopkeepers, knowing that the Poles often did not know enough English, sometimes overcharged them. Although many Poles registered complaints with authorities, they were often ignored.

Not only were these humiliations hard to tolerate, they also undermined the sense

---

The Polish Stereotype

Polish Americans have often borne the brunt of cruel stereotypes that have been reinforced by films, television, and stage productions. One of the most well known Polish stereotypes is that of Stanley Kowalski, created by Tennessee Williams in his play *A Streetcar Named Desire*. The character came to symbolize for many Americans what all Polish American men were like: poorly educated, loud, crude, and heavy drinkers. This image was further reinforced during the early 1970s when the television character of Archie Bunker on *All in the Family* would refer to his Polish American son-in-law, Mike Stivic, as "meathead." For years, too, Polish Americans have been the subject of numerous jokes that made fun of their lower-class background and peasant heritage.

Marlon Brando plays Stanley Kowalski in the film version of A Streetcar Named Desire.

of belonging that Polish immigrants had begun to feel. It also damaged their sense of worth as individuals and as a people. To fight back, Poles from all backgrounds and walks of life united to protect the welfare of their communities and businesses and to assert their dignity.

The Poles battled nativism through the Catholic Church in America, too. For some time Polish clergy had pushed to have their own countrymen placed in higher positions in the church. They succeeded to some extent in 1908 when a Polish priest in Chicago was consecrated as the first Polish bishop of an American city. This was followed by the appointment of another Polish priest into an important church administrative office in Milwaukee in 1914. Polish clergy and laymen also fought with American Roman Catholic Church officials over a policy that recognized English as the official language to be taught in Polish parochial schools. As one Polish cleric argued, "If we forget our Polish heritage we become nothing but ships in the wind without anchors."[60] This struggle would continue for many years before the debate ceased to matter. By that time the number of Polish parochial schools had decreased, as more and more parents sent their children to public schools.

Speaking Through the Ballot Box

If the Polish clergy made advances in church government, many Poles decided that the best way for them to be heard in American society was through the ballot box. Polish participation in American political life was not extensive during the first wave of immigration. Politically, Polish Americans have not been as active in American politics as have other immigrant groups. Their experiences with political oppression in the old country, the language barrier, and the low rate of naturalization among Poles inhibited participation in American politics. As a community they were often more concerned about their own affairs than with those of the nation at large.

Though there were large concentrations of Polish immigrants in nine industrial states, it was not until the 1930s that Poles really became active in the American political process. Still there were signs in the late nineteenth century that Poles were coming to recognize the importance of involvement in local and national politics. During the 1880s and 1890s Poles who had become naturalized American citizens voted according to their allegiance to one of the two large Polish fraternal organizations, the PRCU and the PNA. In general those who belonged to the PRCU tended to support the Democrats, while PNA members voted for Republican candidates.

In some cases Poles joined the Democratic Party because the word *democratic* held a genuine appeal for them. Yet they had more practical reasons for supporting the Democrats. Since the middle of the nineteenth century, the Democrats, more than the Republicans, had been the party of the immigrants and Catholics. The Republican Party, which was founded in the 1850s, contained nativist elements. It seemed to be the party of wealthy, Anglo-Saxon businessmen and routinely excluded immigrants from its ranks. Poles had come to the United States seeking social and economic equality, and the Democrats seemed more supportive of those goals than did their Republican counterparts.

Democratic Party Activists

Many Poles who settled in large cities thus became involved in Democratic "machine" politics. They became part of a political system in which elected officials engaged in such corrupt practices as buying votes and accepting bribes. These officials also provided jobs and services in exchange for support at the polls. This system, though dishonest, was mutually beneficial to both politicians and their constituents. For the politician the system offered the guarantee of votes from various ethnic groups who would otherwise have not participated in politics. For immigrants such as the Poles, machine politics offered patronage, jobs, and a sense of influence within their own communities.

Although they benefited from machine politics, the Poles, unlike the members of other immigrant groups, did not in the long run build on this early success. Compared to other ethnic groups that gained political stature and influence in government, the Poles have never established or maintained long-term political influence or control. Unlike the Irish in Boston or New York, for example, the Poles did not rise to dominate the Democratic political machine. Among the largest ethnic groups in many American cities, Poles have gen-

erally exercised minimal influence on municipal politics.

Polish voters could elect one of their own to the city council or as an alderman, and in fact Polish candidates had resounding success in cities such as Chicago or Cleveland. But rarely did the Poles become judges, chiefs of police, or mayors, even in cities where there were large groups of Polish voters. Poles' frequent refusal to form coalitions with other ethnic groups and their determination to remain isolated and independent cost them opportunities to advance their interests and their candidates. Since the Poles were aloof, others felt no need to reward their loyalty by supporting Polish candidates for office. Not until 1920, for instance, was a Polish American elected to the House of Representatives.

On a national level the Poles did not become a political force until the presidential election of 1928. The Democratic candidate was Alfred E. Smith, a Roman Catholic. Although Smith lost the election to Republican Herbert Hoover, Poles voted overwhelming for Smith. Increasingly Poles have made greater inroads in national politics. By the time of the Great Depression during the 1930s, Polish Americans had become more politically aware and active. For example, the Polish American Democratic Organization (PADO) was formed in 1933 in Chicago. The PADO supported then-president Franklin D. Roosevelt and his New Deal policies, many of which were aimed at helping blue-collar workers get back on their feet. In 1944 the PADO was instrumental in helping reelect Roosevelt to an

The Polish American Congress

In May 1944 a number of Polish Americans met in Buffalo, New York. Out of that meeting came a new political movement, the Polish American Congress (PAC). The organization was created for the express purpose of representing the concerns of Polonia before the government of the United States. Today the Polish American Congress is a federation of more than three thousand Polish American organizations and clubs, including national fraternal benefit societies such as the Polish National Alliance, Polish Women's Alliance, Polish Roman Catholic Union, Polish Falcons, and others, and includes veteran's, cultural, professional, religious, and social associations. The total number of the PAC membership is over 1 million and represents forty-one state divisions and chapters in twenty-three states. The PAC promotes civic, educational, and cultural programs designed not only to further the knowledge of Polish history, language, and culture but to stimulate Polish American involvement and accomplishments.

unprecedented fourth term in office. Though Polish Americans today are more politically diverse than in the past, many remain staunch supporters of the Democratic Party.

Changes and Challenges

By the 1930s Polish American communities throughout the nation were changing rapidly. While the church and the clergy maintained a strong hold on the spiritual and religious life of Polish Americans, other more subtle influences were altering Polish American households and families. Polish American newspapers began to lament how the younger generation, the majority of whom had been born in the United States, no longer seemed interested in their history and heritage. Radio stations that played traditional Polish music and offered Polish programs began to mix in popular American music along with the usual standards. Dances and folksongs, once the mainstay of many Polish households, were now only performed on special occasions. Once so enmeshed in the politics of Poland, the fraternal organizations and associations were now actively involved in local political campaigns and union activities.

In some ways the attitudes of the second-generation Polish Americans mirrored those of their parents and grandparents. Instead of staying in Polonia, many young Poles moved away from the old neighborhoods, sometimes relocating far from home. Those who stayed in Polonia tended more and more to submerge their Polish identity and to assimilate into American culture. Athletic teams, social clubs, professional groups,

The Polka

Of all the dances originating in the nineteenth century, the polka is the only one that has survived. The polka is a lively couple's dance that is originally from Bohemia. Its basic steps were simple, consisting of a hop-step-close-step done in two/four time. After the initial enthusiasm, the polka gradually declined in popularity and reached a low point with the introduction of ragtime, jazz, and the newer dances of the early twentieth century. After the Second World War, however, Polish immigrants to the United States adopted the polka as their "national" dance. There are other forms of Polish dance still practiced today. One is the polonaise, named for its country of origin, which was a stately processional march often used for the opening of a fancy dress ball. However, it never achieved great popularity as a ballroom dance. The Polish mazurka, a fairly complicated dance to waltz music, included hops, sliding steps, and kicking the heels together. But for many Polish Americans the polka is the hands-down favorite with its variable style—from robust to smooth—short-glide steps and ever-happy music. One of the most popular versions of the

polka is called the "heel and toe and away we go" due to its ease in execution. Polka steps are also popular in country and western dance music.

A modern-day polka band performs a lively tune.

and youth organizations focused on the community at large rather than merely on the Polish neighborhood.

Polonia was changing in other ways, too. Although many young Polish Americans might continue to speak Polish at home, especially to parents and grandparents or older aunts and uncles, they were less likely to marry a Pole or to live in the old neighborhood. Born in the United States, the younger generations had, quite naturally, become more American than Polish, and they did not seem overly distressed at the change. They may have known about such Polish figures as Kazimierz (Casimir) Pulaski and Thaddeus Kosciuszko, both Polish heroes of the American Revolution, but chances were better that they could more readily identify with Americans such as George Washington, Thomas Jefferson, Abraham Lincoln, or even Babe Ruth.

Patriots for Poland and America

Second-generation Polish Americans had a growing sense of being "Americans," which translated into a strong sense of nationalism during the two world wars. In general, Polish Americans rallied around the American war efforts. It was, to be sure, easier for them to do so than perhaps it was for some Germans and Italians, whose countries were, at one time or another, the enemies of the United States. The outbreak of the First World War in 1914 heightened anxiety among Polish immigrants, as they watched Poland become a battleground between the Russian and German forces. Adding to the conflict was the drafting of Poles in Europe to fight for either the army of the kaiser (Germany) or the army of the czar (Russia). These divisions played out in Polish American communities. Those whose relatives served in the Russian army favored the czar and the Allied Powers (Great Britain, France, the United States in 1917, along with Russia), while those with family in the German army supported the kaiser and the Central Powers (Germany, Austria-Hungary, and the Ottoman Empire). To gain favor from the United States, both the Allied and the Central Powers promised to create a free and independent Poland at the end of the war.

Polish immigrants were overjoyed at the thought of achieving a free and independent Poland. As the war dragged on into 1915 and 1916 with no end in sight, leaders of the Polish American community called for American involvement to ensure Polish independence. The Polish-language press was one of the most ardent supporters of the United States joining the war. As one Pole noted, the pages of Polish-language newspapers "were filled with emotional appeals for assistance to the 'Fatherland' and interest in Poland's fate became the single most important issue drawing readers to the Polish-language newspaper."[61]

Polonia found other ways to show its support for Poland. The Union of Polish Falcons voted to recruit 1 million Polish volunteers to form the "Army of Kosciuszko," named in honor of the American Revolutionary war hero Thaddeus Kosciuszko who came from Poland to help the American patriots. The American secretary of war, however, rejected the offer. When President Wilson finally committed the United States to combat in April 1917 and called for volunteers, forty thousand of the first one hundred thousand men to report for duty were Polish American. In some Polish American communities every young man of military age joined the armed services.

Rising Against an Old Enemy

In 1939 Polish Americans watched in horror as the Nazis invaded and conquered

Paderewski and Polonia

One of the most influential figures in drumming up support for a free Poland was the famous Polish concert pianist Ignacy Jan Paderewski, who came to the United States in March 1915. It

was Paderewski's hope to raise money to aid Polish war victims and to win the support of the U.S. government in their cause. For the next year Paderewski performed a series of concerts and organized relief efforts for the Polish cause. His efforts were a great success. Both Polish and non-Polish Americans responded to his pleas for help with offers of money and donations. President Woodrow Wilson even proclaimed January 1, 1916, as Polish Relief Day. On this day every Polish American was to donate one day's wages to the Red Cross for aid to Polish victims. Because of Paderewski's efforts, Polonia also came to be called the "Fourth Province of Poland" and for the first time a majority of Americans became aware of a special place called Polonia.

Ignacy Paderewski lobbied for American support of Polish independence during World War I.

Poland in five short weeks. The grief and anger over the fate that had befallen their country rallied Polish Americans to fight against the Nazis. By the time the United States entered the Second World War in December 1941, hundreds of thousands of Polish American men and women had already joined the American military. More than 1 million, or approximately 12 percent of the entire armed forces during the war, were Polish American. The Second World War also marked the first time that a number of Polish American soldiers were promoted to the rank of officer. Polish Americans at home also did their part to support the war effort, participating in activities such as drives to sell war bonds and programs to conserve valuable material and resources, such as oil, gasoline, rubber, and silk. In many homes blue stars hung in windows to denote a loved one serving in uniform; it was not uncommon to find five or six stars in the windows of some Polish American homes. In addition, organizations such as the Polish National Alliance and the Polish Roman Catholic Union raised enough money to cover the cost of five bombers, which were christened with Polish names.

By the end of the war in 1945 approximately thirty thousand Polish Americans had given their lives for the cause. Yet, when Polish American servicemen and servicewomen returned home, they found that some things had not changed. Many were still passed over for jobs because their last names were not "American." As a result many Polish Americans began to change their names, believing that if they concealed their Polish ancestry they could escape discrimination and rise in American society. Older immigrants lamented the loss of another link to their homeland and their past.

Where Are You Going?

Today ongoing challenges confront the Polish American community in the United States, even though Polish immigrants and their descendants have already accomplished much in the land that they have come to call home. But the tensions of maintaining traditional cultural ways and heritage while participating in American society have led to arguments and some divisiveness within the Polish community over the issue of assimilation. For Polish Americans today, the task ahead is how best to incorporate the cultural institutions brought to the United States more than a century ago into modern, American-born Polish communities.

In the meantime Polish Americans continue to make valuable contributions to American society and culture from all walks of life.

Losing Touch?

While many first-generation Poles feared that Polish Americans would become "extinct," census numbers tell a very different story. As the third wave of Polish migration continues into this country even today, there appears to be no shortage of Polish heritage anywhere in America. But perhaps what many of the older Polish immigrants fear most is that the more recent generations of Polish Americans have lost touch with their heritage. Still there are a number of different factors that have weakened the once-strong cultural ties between Poland and American Poles.

These weakened ties were particularly distressing during the years following the Second World War as old and new immigrants faced the challenges of economic uncertainty, dying neighborhoods, and negative images of themselves in the American media. There were also concerns over decreased church attendance, the growing number of Poles marrying non-Poles, and the declining influence of Polish schools. Despite these changes and challenges, there were a number of hopeful signs present in Polonia.

New and Old

With the influx of new immigrants over the last four decades, many Polish traditions have remained intact. However, relations between the old and new immigrants have not always been harmonious. Many of the new arrivals find the older immigrants to be old-fashioned and ignorant. Many of the newer immigrants have also chosen to bypass the older Polonia organizations and associations, instead creating their own, joining more mainstream American groups, or in some cases taking over the more established Polonia groups and forcing older members out. Quite often the new immigrants have refused to take part in Polish American celebrations. By the same token, some older Polish immigrants look upon the new arrivals as "not having paid their dues," criticizing them for being selfish and ashamed of their heritage.

Cool relations also occur because many of the older Poles tend to be from working-class backgrounds, while the new Polish immigrants are more affluent. These differences have led one historian of Polish America to note that there are two very distinct Polonias in America today, "the pretending Polonia of the polonaise and the real Polonia of the polka."[62] Old immigrants also accuse the new immigrants of being "Professional Poles" who pretend to be ethnic while ignoring those older immigrants who uphold the traditional ways.

Polish Pride

In spite of these difficulties, over the years Polish Americans have retained much of their ethnic identity and in fact remain one of the strongest ethnic groups in the United States today. Where the second generation moved away from many of the traditional ways, it is the third and fourth generation of Polish Americans who have "rediscovered" much of their ethnicity and with it a great pride in their culture and heritage.

This renewed interest among Polish Americans beginning in the 1970s was aided by a number of positive role models and events. The name of Polish American Leon Jaworski, who was the special prosecutor during the Watergate investigation of President Richard Nixon, became a household word, as did the appointment of National Security Advisor Zbigniew Brzezinski under President Jimmy Carter.

Some Long-Standing Traditions

Even though the numbers of Polish immigrants in America have declined considerably, Polish culture remains strong and vibrant. The most enduring customs are connected with the traditions of the church. Polish Americans celebrate some special holidays in America as well as traditional holidays such as Christmas and Easter. On Christmas Eve the entire family waits until the youngest child spots the first star of the evening. Then candles are lit and the family sits down to Christmas Eve dinner, known as *wigilia*. The best china and crystal are used for this special meal.

Dinner is served on a white tablecloth under which some straw is scattered. The hay and cloth represent the manger and the veil of Mary that was used to cover the infant Jesus. At the center of the table is placed the *oplatek*, or wafer, which is also placed in a small bed of hay, along with a figure of the Christ child. Tradition also dictates that an empty place be set for an unexpected guest, in memory of ancestors, inviting their spirits to be with the family. This is in keeping with a Polish saying, *Gość w domu, Bóg w domu*," or "Guest in the home is God in the home." The actual meal consists of twelve courses, one for each of the apostles. To ensure good luck, one must taste each course, and there must be an even number of people at the dinner table.

The Tuesday before the beginning of Lent is also a time of celebration in Polish households. It is known as Pączki Day and is named for the fruit-filled doughnuts that Poles enjoy eating. On this day it is common to see lines of people outside Polish bakeries waiting for this delicious treat.

Easter traditionally marked the beginning of the farmer's year and is celebrated with great meals including a variety of meats and cakes, butter molded in the shape of a lamb, and much drinking and dancing. Polish Americans also make *pysanky*, the brightly colored eggs created at Easter, which symbolize Christ's tomb and the resurrection. Another custom, the art of *wycinanki,* or paper cutting, was used to decorate the walls of the home with paper figures traditionally cut with sheep shears. There are two basic kinds of Polish paper cut-outs: one-color symmetrical forms showing forest or woodland scenes, called *leluja*, and multicolor compositions featuring flowers, roosters, or scenes of daily life.

A Polish American man enjoys a fruit-filled pastry known as a pączki. *Polish Americans still eat many of the foods made by their immigrant forebears.*

Events overseas also stirred Polish Americans, including the election of the first Polish pope, Cardinal Karol Wojtyla as Pope John Paul II; the growth of the Polish workers' movement, Solidarity, which helped hasten the end of communism; and the awarding of the Nobel Peace Prize to Lech Walesa, the head of Solidarity and the first president of Poland after the fall of the communist regime.

At the same time many Americans now had the opportunity to learn more about Poland, thanks to a growing interest by colleges and universities in creating Slavic studies programs. The Library of Congress sponsored a successful exhibit of Polish folklore, and in general there was a heightened interest in Polish poster art, literature, theater, and film throughout the country.

Giving Back to America

Polish Americans have made a number of valuable contributions to American life. Among the most famous of these individuals are Maria Goeppert Mayer, who shared the 1963 Nobel Prize in physics for her contributions to research on the shell model of the atomic nucleus, and Casimir Funk, a biochemist who was the first to use the term *vitamin*. Dr. Stanley Dudrick is credited with developing one of the most important technologies in medicine, the intravenous hyperalimention, or IHA, which provides nourishment and medicine to the body through the veins.

In the field of the fine arts Polish Americans are well represented. Virtuoso pianist Artur Rubinstein was awarded the U.S. Medal of Freedom in 1976. One of the world's most famous conductors,

Maurice Sendak is a well-known Polish American author and illustrator of children's books.

Leopold Stokowski, became a U.S. citizen in 1915 and one of this country's leading conductors as well as being credited with helping to popularize classical music for millions of Americans.

Maurice Sendak, illustrator and writer of children's books, is of Polish descent, as was Isaac Bashevis Singer, Polish American writer and recipient of the 1978 Nobel Prize for literature. Jules Feiffer, known for his biting political cartoons, is also Polish American.

The world of film has been deeply touched by Polish Americans. Harry and Jack Warner were the sons of Polish immigrants and went on to create Warner Brothers Studios, one of the most successful film studios in Hollywood. One of Hollywood's most successful producers, directors, and screenwriters was Joseph L. Mankiewicz, who helped bring to the screen such classics as *The Philadelphia Story* and *All About Eve*. Mankiewicz's brother Herman, who was a screenwriter, won an Oscar for the film *Citizen Kane*, considered one of the greatest films ever made.

Polish Americans have continued to make inroads into the political sphere as well. One of the most respected Polish American

Two Boys of Summer

While a number of Polish Americans have excelled at the American sport of baseball, two figures have commanded special attention for their skills. Stan Musial, also known as "Stan the Man," became one of the top players in National League history. Playing for the St. Louis Cardinals, Musial won the Most Valuable Player award three times. His career spanned twenty-two years—from 1941 to 1963—and in 1969 he was elected to the Baseball Hall of Fame. Carl Yastrzemski, who joined the Boston Red Sox in 1961, was also selected for induction into the Hall of Fame. "Yaz," as he was known, was also one of the best all-around baseball players of his time. In 1967 he made history by capturing the "Triple Crown," leading the American League in home runs, runs batted in, and batting average. He also led the Red Sox to the World Series that season.

Stan Musial (left) and Carl Yastrzemski pose with their bats. Both Polish American baseball players enjoyed record-setting careers.

presidential candidate on the Democratic ticket in 1968 with Hubert Humphrey. In 1972 Muskie considered a bid for the presidency, but his campaign floundered. He continued to play an active role in politics for many years thereafter. Barbara Mikulski and Dan Rostenkowski are two other Polish Americans who have successfully won political office. Mikulski is a Democratic senator from Maryland; Rostenkowski served in the House of Representatives as the Democratic representative from Illinois, and for many years chaired the powerful House Ways and Means Committee.

In the world of business and commerce Polish Americans have made numerous contributions. Oleg Cassini became known in fashion circles for his inventive designs, while Ruth Handler, the cofounder of the Mattel Toy Company and creator of the Barbie doll, is the daughter of Polish immigrants. Leo Gerstenzang, a Polish immigrant from Warsaw, was the inventor of the cotton swab.

Pope John Paul II blesses Polish American girls in New York. Most Polish Americans remain devout Catholics, and church attendance is very high throughout Polonia.

politicians was Edmund Muskie, who became the first Polish American governor of Maine and later its first Polish American senator. Muskie also ran as a vice

Is There Still a Polonia?

Even with this renewed interest in the Polish heritage Polonia has been undergoing changes. Church attendance remains high, but now masses are said in English. While Polonia's Catholic Church once viewed the preservation of Polish heritage and culture among its duties, churches in Polish American neighborhoods now reach out to other ethnic groups. This also reflects the changing face of Polonia's neighborhoods, which are becoming more ethnically and racially mixed. Still, approximately 76 percent of Polish parishes nationwide are still active.

The parochial schools of Polonia have also fallen victim to the times. As Poles moved away from the neighborhood, attendance in the schools decreased, and the schools found it harder and harder to stay open. With costs increasing and the number of students decreasing, many schools closed.

However, in other areas of education, the prospects are much brighter. More Poles are now not only finishing high school, but many are going on to college. Today Polish Americans rank above the national average in the number of years of schooling and in the acquisition of college degrees. According to 1990 census reports of Polish Americans between the age of eighteen and twenty-five, 85.8 percent have high school diplomas compared with the national average of 78.7 percent. In the same age group, 11.4 percent of Polish Americans have received college degrees compared with the national average of 7.6 percent.

Although these strides are heartening, it has taken longer for Poles to progress in the area of jobs. More Polish Americans are now doing jobs requiring a professional or technical education. According to the 1990 census 49 percent of Polish Americans hold a bachelor's degree or higher. According to the 2000 census Polish Americans have a median annual household income of $45,800. The same census reports that 56 percent of Polish Americans are married, with an average number of 1.5 children in their families. Fewer than 4 percent of Polish American families live in poverty compared to the national average of 10 percent.

It is clear that the Polonia that survives today is a very different one from the community founded over a century ago by the first wave of Polish immigrants. But in order to survive, today's Polish Americans need to confront more readily the concerns of their community and not just those of Poland. And perhaps more important, Polish Americans might want to remember the promise of their heritage as outlined in an essay written in the 1950s. The author, a young Polish American, outlined why he was proud to be Polish:

I am proud that I am a Pole—and for good reasons. My Polish ancestry entitles me to a share in a history that is rich in God-fearing heroes and heroines, who have championed the cause of liberty, peace, and freedom; of honesty and justice; of equality and brotherhood. Polish descent offers a heritage of honor . . . . Yes, I am proud to be a Pole—for a good Pole has every right and reason to be a good American.[63]

NOTES

Introduction: A Second Polish History

1. Quoted in Bogdan Grzeloński, ed., *America Through Polish Eyes: An Anthology.* Warsaw, Poland: Interpress, 1988, p. 236.
2. Quoted in John J. Bukowczyk, ed., "Polish Americans, History Writing, and the Organization of Memory," in *Polish Americans and Their History: Community, Culture, and Politics.* Pittsburgh: University of Pittsburgh Press, 1996, p. 1.

Chapter One: *Stary Kraj* (The Old Country)

3. Quoted in Shirley Blumenthal, *Coming to America: Immigrants from Eastern Europe.* New York: Delacorte, 1981, p. 12.
4. Quoted in Blumenthal, *Coming to America*, p. 14.

Chapter Two: Looking Across the Ocean

5. Quoted in James Pula, *Polish Americans: An Ethnic Community.* New York: Twayne, 1995, p. 17.
6. Quoted in Pula, *Polish Americans*, p. 15.
7. Quoted in John J. Bukowczyk, *And My Children Did Not Know Me: A History of the Polish-Americans.* Bloomington: Indiana University Press, 1987, p. 1.
8. Quoted in Bukowczyk, *And My Children Did Not Know Me*, p. 14.
9. Quoted in W.S. Kuniczak, *My Name Is Million: An Illustrated History of the Poles in America.* New York: Hippocrene Books, 2000, p. 171.
10. Quoted in Blumenthal, *Coming to America*, p. 70.
11. Quoted in Bukowczyk, *And My Children Did Not Know Me*, p. 17.
12. Quoted in Blumenthal, *Coming to America*, p. 70.
13. Quoted in Blumenthal, *Coming to America*, p. 65.
14. Quoted in Blumenthal, *Coming to America*, p. 65.

Chapter Three: To America

15. Quoted in Pula, *Polish Americans*, p. 17.
16. Quoted in Bruce M. Stave and John F. Sutherland, with Aldo Salerno, *From the Old Country: An Oral History of European Migration to America.* New York: Twayne, 1994, pp. 26–27.
17. Quoted in David M. Brownstone, Irene M. Franck, and Douglass Brownstone, *Island of Hope, Island of Tears.* New York: Barnes & Noble, 2000, p. 29.
18. Quoted in Brownstone, et al., *Island of Hope, Island of Tears*, p. 39.
19. Quoted in Brownstone, et al., *Island of Hope, Island of Tears*, pp. 54–55.
20. Quoted in Brownstone, et al., *Island of Hope, Island of Tears*, pp. 39–40.
21. Quoted in Ivan Chermayeff, Fred Wasserman, and Mary J. Shapiro, *Ellis Island: An Illustrated History of the Immigrant Experience.* New York: Macmillan, 1991, p. 39.

22. Quoted in Mary Shapiro, *Gateway to Liberty: The Story of the Statue of Liberty and Ellis Island*. New York: Vintage Books, 1986, p. 97.

23. Quoted in Chermayeff, et al., *Ellis Island*, p. 37.

Chapter Four:
The Golden Door to America

24. Quoted in Brownstone, et al., *Island of Hope, Island of Tears*, p. 142.

25. Quoted in Brownstone, et al., *Island of Hope, Island of Tears*, p. 144.

26. Quoted in Brownstone, et al., *Island of Hope, Island of Tears*, p. 155.

27. Quoted in Brownstone, et al., *Island of Hope, Island of Tears*, p. 155.

28. Quoted in Brownstone, et al., *Island of Hope, Island of Tears*, p. 157.

29. Quoted in Shapiro, *Gateway to Liberty*, p. 158.

30. Quoted in Brownstone, et al., *Island of Hope, Island of Tears*, p. 177.

31. Quoted in Brownstone, et al., *Island of Hope, Island of Tears*, pp. 192–93.

32. Quoted in Brownstone, et al., *Island of Hope, Island of Tears*, p. 179.

33. Quoted in Brownstone, et al., *Island of Hope, Island of Tears*, p. 240.

34. Quoted in Shapiro, *Gateway to Liberty*, p. 170.

Chapter Five: To Work

35. Quoted in Pula, *Polish Americans*, p. 20.

36. Quoted in Bukowczyk, *And My Children Did Not Know Me*, p. 21.

37. Quoted in Pula, *Polish Americans*, p. 46.

38. Quoted in Blumenthal, *Coming to America*, p. 111.

39. Quoted in Kuniczak, *My Name Is Million*, p. 172.

40. Quoted in Bukowczyk, *And My Children Did Not Know Me*, p. 16.

41. Quoted in Bukowczyk, *And My Children Did Not Know Me*, p. 26.

42. Quoted in Blumenthal, *Coming to America*, pp. 95–96.

43. Quoted in Pula, *Polish Americans, p.* 47.

44. Quoted in Kuniczak, *My Name Is Million*, p. 171.

45. Quoted in Pula, *Polish Americans*, pp. 50–51.

46. Quoted in Blumenthal, *Coming to America*, p. 92.

47. Quoted in Kuniczak, *My Name Is Million*, p. 172.

Chapter Six: Polonia

48. Quoted in Kuniczak, *My Name Is Million*, p. 171.

49. Quoted in Pula, *Polish Americans, p.* 30.

50. Quoted in Pula, *Polish Americans*, pp. 30–31.

51. Quoted in Pula, *Polish Americans*, p. 37.

52. Quoted in Pula, *Polish Americans*, p. 26.

53. Quoted in Bukowczyk, *And My Children Did Not Know Me*, p. 97.

Chapter Seven: Trying to Fit In

54. Quoted in Blumenthal, *Coming to America*, p. 162.

55. Quoted in Bukowczyk, *And My Children Did Not Know Me*, p. 67.

56. Quoted in Blumenthal, *Coming to America*, p. 166.

57. Quoted in Blumenthal, *Coming to America*, p. 169.

58. Desmond S. King, *Making Americans: Immigration, Race, and the Origins of the Diverse Democracy*. Cambridge, MA: Harvard University Press, 2000, p. 51.

59. Quoted in Bukowczyk, *And My Chil-dren Did Not Know Me,* p. 68.

60. Quoted in Bukowczyk, *And My Chil-dren Did Not Know Me,* p. 69.

61. Quoted in Bukowczyk, *And My Chil-dren Did Not Know Me,* p. 55.

Epilogue: Where Are You Going?

62. Quoted in Pula, *Polish Americans,* p. 138.

63. Quoted in Bukowczyk, *And My Chil-dren Did Not Know Me,* p. 146.

FOR FURTHER READING

Books

Sean Dolan, *The Polish Americans*. Philadelphia: Chelsea House, 1996. An overview of the history and culture of Polish Americans.

Sharon Moscinski, *Tracing Our Polish Roots*. New York: Avalon Travel, 1994. A history of Poland and Polish immigration.

Lucia Raatma, *Polish Americans*. New York: Child's World, 2002. An overview of the Poles in America.

Carl Sokolnicki Rollyson and Lisa Olson Paddock, *A Student's Guide to Polish American Genealogy*. New York: Oryx Press, 1996. A historical and cultural overview of Poland with a special emphasis on the contributions and heritage of Polish Americans.

Conrad R. Stein, *Ellis Island*. Chicago: Childrens Press, 1992. Brief history of Ellis Island.

Rachel Toor, *The Polish Americans*. Philadelphia: Chelsea House, 1988. A history of Poles in the United States.

Periodicals

Cobblestone Magazine, May 1995. This entire issue is devoted to the history and culture of Polish Americans.

WORKS CONSULTED

Books

Shirley Blumenthal, *Coming to America: Immigrants from Eastern Europe.* New York: Delacorte Press, 1981. Among the immigrant groups covered in this book are the Poles.

David M. Brownstone, Irene M. Franck, and Douglass Brownstone, *Island of Hope, Island of Tears.* New York: Barnes & Noble, 2000. First-person accounts of immigrant experiences at Ellis Island and in America.

John J. Bukowczyk, *And My Children Did Not Know Me: A History of the Polish-Americans.* Bloomington: Indiana University Press, 1987. A concise history of Polish immigration to the United States.

———, ed., *Polish Americans and Their History, Community, Culture, and Politics.* Pittsburgh: University of Pittsburgh Press, 1996. A collection of essays about Polish Americans.

Ivan Chermayeff, Fred Wasserman, and Mary J. Shapiro, *Ellis Island: An Illustrated History of the Immigrant Experience.* New York: Macmillan, 1991. A pictorial history of Ellis Island.

Roger Daniels, *Coming to America: A History of Immigration and Ethnicity in American Life.* New York: HarperCollins, 1990. A broad overview chronicling the history of American immigration.

Norman Davies, *Heart of Europe: A Short History of Poland.* New York: Oxford University Press, 1986. A concise history of Poland.

Bogdan Grzeloński, ed., *America Through Polish Eyes: An Anthology.* Warsaw, Poland: Interpress, 1988. A collection of first-person accounts written about America by Poles.

Melvin G. Holli and Peter d'A. Jones, *Ethnic Chicago.* Grand Rapids, MI: William B. Eerdmans, 1984. Includes a chapter on Polish Americans in Chicago.

Desmond S. King, *Making Americans: Immigration, Race, and the Origins of the Diverse Democracy.* Cambridge, MA: Harvard University Press, 2000. A discussion of how 1920s U.S. immigration policy played an important role in shaping democracy and influencing ideas about ethnic groups.

W.S. Kuniczak, *My Name Is Million: An Illustrated History of the Poles in America.* New York: Hippocrene Books, 2000. A pictorial history of the Polish immigrant in America.

Ann Novotny, *Strangers at the Door: Ellis Island, Castle Garden, and the Great Migration to America.* Riverside, CT: Chatham Press, 1971. A good history of Ellis Island with numerous firsthand accounts.

James Pula, *Polish Americans: An Ethnic Community.* New York: Twayne, 1995. A history of Polish Americans.

Frank Renkiewicz, ed., *Poles in America, 1608–1972.* Dobbs Ferry, NY: Oceana Publications, 1973. A history of

Polish emigration to the United States, arranged chronologically.

Mary Shapiro, *Gateway to Liberty: The Story of the Statue of Liberty and Ellis Island.* New York: Vintage Books, 1986. The sections on Ellis Island provide a history of the institution and include many first-person accounts.

Bruce M. Stave and John F. Sutherland, with Aldo Salerno, *From the Old Country: An Oral History of European Migration to America.* New York: Twayne, 1994. A collection of first-person accounts from immigrants, including Poles.

Wilton S. Tifft, *Ellis Island.* Chicago: Contemporary Books, 1989. A history of Ellis Island, including first-person accounts of immigrants who came through.

Virginia Yans-McLaughlin and Marjorie Lightman, with the Statue of Liberty–Ellis Island Foundation, *Ellis Island and the Peopling of America: The Official Guide.* New York: New Press, 1990. A history of and resource guide for Ellis Island.

Websites

The Kosciuszko Foundation (www.kosciuszkofoundation.org). This is the official site for the Kosciuszko Foundation.

The Polish American Center (www.polishamericancenter.org). The official site for the Organization to Preserve Polish Culture.

The Polish American Association (www.polish.org). This site features a youth page.

Polish Art Center: Treasury of Polish Heritage (www.polartcenter.com). Distributes books, Polish-made dolls, crafts, jewelry, and other items. Also contains a guide to traditional Polish holidays and customs.

INDEX

PICTURE CREDITS

ABOUT THE AUTHOR

Meg Greene, the great-granddaughter of Polish immigrants, is a writer and historian with degrees in history and historic preservation. She is also a contributing editor to "History for Children," for Suite 101.com. Ms. Greene makes her home in Virginia.